DISCOURSE IN THE SOCIAL SCIENCES

DISCOURSE IN THE SOCIAL SCIENCES

STRATEGIES FOR TRANSLATING MODELS OF MENTAL ILLNESS

Jonathan D. Moreno

and

Barry Glassner

Contributions in Sociology, Number 40

GREENWOOD PRESS
Westport, Connecticut · London, England

Library of Congress Cataloging in Publication Data

Moreno, Jonathan D.
  Discourse in the social sciences.

  (Contributions in sociology, ISSN 0084-9278; no. 40)
  Includes bibliographical references and index.
  1. Psychology, Pathological—Philosophy. 2. Psychology,
Pathological—Language 3. Social sciences—
Language. I. Glassner, Barry. II. Title. III. Series.
RC437.5.M65   157'.01'4   81–7092
ISBN 0-313-23159-1 (lib. bdg.)   AACR2

First published in 1982

Greenwood Press
A division of Congressional Information Service, Inc.
88 Post Road West, Westport, Connecticut 06881

Printed in the United States of America

10 9 8 7 6 5 4 3 2 1

to Jyoti and Leslye,
our translators

Les langues imparfaites en cela que plusiers, manque la suprème: penser étant écrire sans accessoires, ni chuchotement mais tacite encore l'im-mortelle parole, la diversité, sur terre, des idiomes empêche personne de proférer les mots qui, sinon se trouveraient, par une frappe unique, elle-même matériellement la vérité.

Mallarmé

The imperfection of languages consists in their plurality, the supreme one is lacking: thinking is writing without accessories or even whispering, the immortal word still remains silent; the diversity of idioms on earth prevents everybody from uttering the words which otherwise, at one single stroke, would materialize as truth.

Translation by Benjamin

Contents

Acknowledgments

The authors wish to thank, for their careful attention to earlier drafts of the manuscript, and for their helpful comments, Wayne Davis, Robert Feleppa, C. V. Haldipur, Stipe Mestrovic, Manfred Stanley, David Sylvan, and Stephen Turner. We also thank our colleagues in the Department of Philosophy at George Washington University and the Department of Sociology at Syracuse University, for their support and assistance. Our editor, Bill Gum, has been an asset to the project from even before it began.

The order of names of the authors was determined arbitrarily; the authors contributed equally in preparation of the manuscript.

DISCOURSE
IN THE SOCIAL
SCIENCES

Can Models Be Translated?

Social scientists occasionally organize symposia or sections of journals in which persons from disparate conceptual or theoretical camps discuss an issue. Sometimes the topic concerns proper procedures for clinical practice, sometimes an empirical finding, and other times the present state of theory development. Whether the debate is between behaviorists and Freudians, Marxists and sociobiologists, or any other such pairing, the audience attraction for such events is likely to be the inevitability that participants will do battle: at worst by name calling, at best by arguments over relative superiority of positions. If the events of this sort that we have witnessed are representative, the most likely outcome is that each side will conclude that they were right from the start, that their own views really are superior. If the participants are among the more secure or receptive social scientists, a point or two made by the opposition will result in rethinking of part of their position, or even of incorporations into their own work of some of the views or findings that the other body of thought has to offer.

If one asks the participants or the audience why so little agreement was reached, or why the parties insist upon talking so differently about a given question, the answer is a straightforward, "because their theories are so different," or if a partisan is responding, "because that other theory is so poor." If one goes further, and seeks from the social scientific literature some carefully argued positions, the situation does not improve very much.

In the papers and discussions from a conference on theories of psychology,[1] for instance, impressive attempts were made to suggest ways in which the disparate theories could be unified, or at least analyzed in a metascientific way, to reveal what is at issue in each. Toward the middle of the book that resulted from the conference William Rozebloom concluded: "There has been an awful lot of unnecessary controversy in which psychologists have shouted at each other without having any substantive bone of contention—what is likely to emerge under analysis is that each combatant is outraged (perhaps with some justice) by the other's metaphors, doesn't think that the other is concerned with the right issues, and has grossly distorted the content of the other's position. Conversely, I strongly suspect that there is considerably more substantive agreement among manifestly conflicting psychologies than is generally realized."[2]

On Rozebloom's account, and many have agreed with his assessment, psychology's theorists are poor or unwilling listeners to one another. In a recent paper, Nicholas Tatsis[3] has poked fun at sociologists along similar lines. Tatsis characterizes sociologists' attempts to communicate between sociological "languages" as variously esoteric, transgressive, reductionistic, integrationist. He contends that when a sociologist tries to use the works of another, he will change the other's statements to show that these work better in his language than in the other's, or will simplify the other's language with an iconoclastic rewording, or else will try to harmonize two ways of talking. The results are inevitably disheartening, according to Tatsis' reading of a variety of such communications.

> With great sensitivity, every sociologist followed his own theoretical vocabulary. This purism is more significant in some intralingual translations where we witness a kind of contemporary scholasticism. Words are sacred for they have already become guardians of meaning.... The translations indicated that contrary to other forms of discourse sociology is dominated by polyglottism. Despite their irreconcilable differences, sociologists seem to accept this polyglottism as the natural course of events. As far as we could determine, no one has yet investigated the consequences of this polyglottism in the fragmentation of sociological experience, the conception of reality, the educational system, the confusion caused by the absence of a mother-tongue, and the handicap in relation to the natural scientists who speak only one language.[4]

In psychiatry the situation is apparently no better. We have been able to find very few examples of persons discussing matters between theories or utilizing the findings of schools of thought other than their own. Theorists and researchers often publish in journals devoted to their own way of looking (compare *The Psychoanalytic Review* with *International Pharmacopsychiatry*). Although some general journals continue to present papers from a wide variety of perspectives, not infrequently the mainstream journals will emphasize one model over another for several years. A few decades ago, journals included a great deal of material from psychonanalysts; more recently they have emphasized biochemical investigations. Sometimes the history of psychiatry is written in this way, as when Ronald Fieve talks about the chemical revolution replacing the Freudian revolution.[5]

This book will examine in a particular way this often noted problem of communication between schools in the social sciences, by considering how conceptual systems importantly differ. Our goal is to suggest strategies to prevent *un*important differences from hindering communication between theorists, and to promote cumulation of knowledge across the systems of thought. We will suggest that, in many cases, theorists, researchers, and clinicians can utilize insights from "rival" systems in building their own models and theories, and without sacrificing the integrity of their own work. For purposes of illustration we will concentrate upon models of mental illness.

We choose this arena both because in it is a profound diversity of ontological commitments, and because within it echo intimations that some accounts exhaust the territory. The range of proposed models includes strictly biochemical to fully sociocultural, "sick" to problems-in-living, and mentalistic to behavioristic. One side claims that "a psychotic episode is a socio-political event and not a medical incident,"[6] another that "the medical model is the best choice for those suffering from schizophrenia."[7] Further, our own research on mental illness has provided a familiarity with these models and debates.

The burden of this book is to provide strategies that will permit theorists to build upon one another's works, even if those theorists do not accept or understand one another's views. To this end we recommend translation procedures, meant in the usual (nonmetaphorical) sense, whereby messages from one theory may be examined in the vocabulary and way of speaking of another theory.

Very generally, there are two kinds of differences between natural languages: linguistic and cultural. Languages use different words and grammars, and they attend to the world in different ways depending upon the cultures in which they arose. Two sorts of differences exist between theories as well, namely, disparate concepts and ontologies. Various theories use distinct technical terms and also attend to different objects in the world, or to different aspects of the same objects. Psychoanalysts use phrases like "ego development" and "denial defense," and they concentrate upon consciousness as well as behaviors; while behaviorists talk of "reinforcement schedules" and "acquired behavioral dispositions," and deny the reality of consciousness while basing arguments upon behaviors.

With Dell Hymes[8] we can distinguish several levels of linguistic methods of ethnography to indicate what is freighted in our use of "translation." Hymes distinguishes five such levels, from "facilitating," the least ambitious in some respects, to "foundations." A facilitating role for linguistic method provides access to a community, "for survival and rapport with it"; on the other extreme, a foundational role finds the linguistic method relevant to the study of culture as a whole, beyond language itself. Our translations between models are meant to be facilitative in Hymes' sense, thus severely limiting our obligations or expectations concerning the role of our method in other regions of the "culture" of the model.

Our moves to translate between these ways of talking and looking will be seen, we hope, not as an attempt to minimize or distort any extant theory, but in the true spirit of translations. A primary goal of the translators, at least since the first translations of religious works, has been to release important messages from the bondage of their local obscurity and idiosyncrasies, in order that these be available to more of the world. In a manner that is more modest only because at present it is less confident in its details, we wish to translate between models in the social sciences for the same reasons that persons translate great literature or philosophy, because we do not accept the proposition that the existence of several ways of words must stand in the way of communication. A culture is enriched by translations of great works from another culture, and a theory is enriched by translations of insightful observations from other theories. "Language is a constant creation of alternative worlds," George Steiner[9] writes. "In every fixed definition there is obsolescence or failed insight.... Each different tongue offers its own denial of determinism. 'The world,' it says, 'can be other'." Yet, through translation, one develops not a heap of contrary views, but a vehicle for reaching closer to agreement about the nature of things, where that is warranted. "The translater enriches his tongue by allowing the source language to penetrate and modify it. But he does more: he extends his native idiom towards the hidden absolute of meaning."[10]

One need not be a romantic to accept Steiner's point. In the case of translations between models, if such translation is possible, the arguments or conclusions derived from one mode of observation and discourse can be checked, after translation, within another theoretical worldview. The norms of science require continual validation and better specification of findings. In the case of social scientific theories the norms are met through intratheoretic validation, but intertheoretic progress has been preempted by the absence of traffic between theoretical schools.

Despite these benefits, translations have often been suspect, and we expect that objections to translations of models will bear marked resemblances to those that have been offered against natural language translations. For centuries translation has been feared because the beauty or revelatory power of language is said to be sacrificed in translation. In religious and secular attacks alike critics speak of translation as profanation of sacred texts, though in the secular works the profanation is of a special kind: the conversion of a special text into work that is at best mundane.[11] At the heart of the criticism may be a fear of the interpretation inherent in translation. No translation consists simply of the transfer of meaning from one set of symbols to another. In every case the translator must reconcile the different views or ways of talking about the world between the languages and interpret how a peace can be made between the two. In this process the original text undergoes a scrutiny not unlike that of criticism, where it is read and reread, always in light of the concerns and modes of discourse of persons partly outside its own school.[12]

We respond to these general fears of the loss of one's essence in two ways. Most profoundly, one of the two translation strategies we will propose in Chapter 3 operates by making transfers from one model to another on the basis of the essential components of each model. In this method the translator attempts to work from the very foundations of the models in order to perform his task. Quite separately, however, we would point out that those whose tongues we translate are themselves translators. Heine's characterization of the translator's attempt to capture the beauty of the original poem, as "strawplaiting sunbeams," was answered by Poggiolo, who pointed out that the original poem is a translation "of the heavenly music that many can no longer hear in the noisy chaos of this world".[13] In the case of modelers in the social sciences the original authors are literally translators, or at least interpreters, who take the words and actions of persons and groups, and place these in the vocabulary of theories. The person who wheezes and has difficulty breathing when sexually excited might be suspected of "olfactory eroticism" by the psychoanalytic modeler, of "asthma" by the medical modeler, and of "a problem in living" by the Szaszian modeler. We assume that all models are designed on the basis of some experience, even if it is largely with a theory in a related context, and that this experience is interpreted.

Any movement from an observation to communication about that observation is of the same order as the movement from source language to host language. In both cases the task is to understand the original material in such a way that it can be fit into a new system. Within a given model, persons accomplish an intralingual operation that is similar to the interlingual operations we will propose. They speak to one another of the world, and even compare how they see and speak of the world. This claim and its technical implications will be considered in detail in this study.

Some philosophers and social scientists would argue, nevertheless, that translation is impossible or severely limited at the intertheoretic level. On various relativist grounds they suggest that talk about the world is context-specific. Herbert Blumer, a leading symbolic interactionist, combines a kind of idealism and indeterminism to conclude that "objects have no fixed status except as their meaning is sustained through indications and definitions that people make of the object." He proposes that across contexts objects change, that "a star in the sky is a very different object to a modern astrophysicist than it was to a shepherd of biblical times."[14] The relativist position is carried even further in ethnomethodology, where proponents contend that scientific accounts of the social world are to be understood in quite the same way as any other accounts. The goal is to investigate how accounts are produced and to what ends they are used; their modes of production and use being what gives them their rational character. The originator of ethnomethodology, Harold Garfinkel, has proposed that "inquiries of every imaginable kind, from divination to theoretical physics, claim our interest as socially organized artful practices."[15] Combined with the claim that every social setting is to be understood as independently self-organizing with respect to how and about what it makes rational statements, it would appear that translation is ruled out, on the ground that statements make sense only within local contexts.

A similar conclusion is reached, though by a different route, in the work of Peter Winch.[16] Here it is argued that persons play language games, and if we are to understand any given concept or statement we must understand its role in its particular language game—in the complex of actions, interests, and rules that make up the form of life within which it is spoken. Unlike Blumer and Garfinkel, Winch does not extend his thesis about social life in general to include social scientific theories, but presumably beliefs in *any* system of thought are to be understood by way of how they operate within that system. From such a perspective it is hard to see how translators can function successfully.

Independent of how well these positions hold up in general, in the case of translations between models of mental illness there is an obvious retort. In an important regard the various models are not different "forms of life" of separate social settings, because all are involved in the enterprise of explaining madness, all are within Western culture, all are within social science and the developing Western scientific tradition. One may want to deny the position of Walter Benjamin and other universalists about language—that "languages are not strangers to one another, but are, a priori and apart from all historical relationships, interrelated in what they want to express"[17]—on the grounds that primitive and scientific cultures are quite different or that within a society groups vary tremendously in their uses of language. But surely there are overlaps in projects, such as the promotion of emotional well-being, and words, such as "depression," between the models of mental illness, since these models developed for the most part in a single culture and a single century.

The Incommensurability Thesis

This easy way out of the problem does not suffice, however, in light of considerations sparked by developments in epistemology, philosophy of language, and history and philosophy of science during the past two decades. In order to apply some of the results of this literature to our preliminary remarks, we should point out a range of interpretations of the original notion that there are difficulties in the existence of different models of madness. Included in this range are the following propositions:

A. The different models of madness sometimes lead us to disagree on some, but not all, questions of etiology, epidemiology, pathology, therapy, and nosology.
B. The different models of madness lead us to disagree on all counts, so that with regard to any basic principle in one model an advocate of another model will deny that principle.
C. The different models of madness lead us to utterly different descriptions of psychopathological conditions, so different that a description of a certain

phenomenon couched in the terms of one model could not possibly mean the same thing as a description of the same phenomenon couched in the terms of another model.

Interpretation A, while plausible, needs expansion in order to be of interest, since as it stands there is no reason that occasional disagreements among models cannot be solved by the ordinary apparatus of experimental science rather than by dumping all models for the sake of one. However, A does embed an idea we want to defend, namely that the models do not map out entirely exclusive ontological territory, that there are actual regions of overlap among them; so later on A will in effect be resurrected in a more favorable context.

Interpretation B is interesting but false: Even if we knew how to distinguish "basic principles" in a model from others, there is no reason whatsoever that an advocate of one model would necessarily disagree with the basic principles of all others. I can hold x to be true and you can hold not-x to be true, but as to a third party's defense of y, neither of us need have anything to say at all. It seems that interpretation C reflects the more extreme position on the differences among the various models of mental illness, though, as we shall see, it is itself somewhat elusive of precise interpretation.

Let us call interpretation C the incommensurability thesis (IT). The general nature of IT will be addressed later, after we examine further its particular relevance for comparing models of madness. Consider a situation in which several psychotherapists each hold their own model of mental illness, each of which subsumes unique principles of etiology, pathology, treatment, and so on. Now, in this view, the commitment of a practitioner to a particular model is not a matter of evidence but rather one of "faith," for each model promises to resolve remaining theoretical problems in its own terms. No problem necessarily dictates the abandonment of a model, but sometimes a problem is in fact regarded as so intractable, an "anomoly" for the model, that the original model is replaced with another that is regarded as invulnerable on that issue. But his shift in allegiance, too, is not supposed to be derived by reason but by faith, a loss of faith in the old model and a gain of faith in the new one.[18]

Now what is the logical relationship between the models under conditions so described? It cannot be one of logical incompatibility, because this implies that they contradict one another. But if the models contradicted one another we could devise tests, at least in principle, that could produce results to confirm the hypotheses derived from one and disconfirm those derived from the others. However, this is obviously not what is being claimed. Instead, the claim must be that the models cannot be measured against one another at all, that choice among them is a matter of faith, not reason. They are not merely empirically underdetermined, but incomparable. If two or more expressions cannot be measured against one another even though they purport to describe the same phenomenon, they must *mean* utterly different things, so different that there is just no ground for comparison. This, of course, is the point of our interpretation C.

Considering the present rather limited degree of conceptual agreement in psychotherapy, this reading of the situation has an intuitive appeal. Among other things it seems to explain the apparently unreasonable tenacity with which proponents of one approach hold their position against all competitors. But surely any view that suggests that scientific research is founded on faith beyond the usual inductive leaps at least deserves careful scrutiny, for in that case the difference between science and religion becomes quite difficult to make out. And there lies an extraordinary problem for the legitimacy of scientific belief, rendering it epistemologically indistinguishable from the most unreasonably held dogmatism.

In that light we return to a fuller characterization of interpretation C, one suggested by Siegler and Osmond's adoption of Thomas S. Kuhn's "paradigm" thesis of scientific revolution.[19] Let us compress the original Kuhnian thesis into the following statements. Paradigms, as understood by Kuhn, function in such a way as to permit the continuation of "normal science": Research based on past scientific achievements acknowledged by the scientific community as the foundation for future practice.[20] The rules governing normal science are shared, often unconsciously, by the practitioners, who sometimes come to understand the rules of that particular game independently[21] of one another. On this account, at some point in the pursuit of normal science there emerges an "anomoly," a fact or a number of facts that resists integration into the regnant paradigm. Then the community may be thrust into a period highlighted by debates about appropriate epistemological principles for that discipline. If a new paradigm emerges, it is embraced by those who have a kind of conversion experience, for they undergo something like a Gestalt switch that allows them to "see" the veracity and fecundity of the new paradigm.[22]

On the reading of this problem it is not just that the old paradigm and the new one are incompatible, but rather that they are *incommensurable*.[23] If they were incompatible they would at least be translatable into each other's terms *and* be talking about the same thing, for unless both these conditions were met we could never even know when they were inconsistent. Consider the French housepainter who, pointing to a wall says, "il est bleu," and his somewhat color-blind American co-worker who responds, "It is green." Only because they could learn to speak the same language *and* because there really is something that could be taken to be a wall that is there for them to disagree about, can the two wallviews be measured against each other. But if one or both of these conditions is not met, then there is no ground for adjudicating the dispute because, in an important sense, there is no common context of meaning. Notice that in the event the latter condition is not met the former condition could still be met, although no amelioration of the disagreement could be achieved.

Kuhn believes that at least one of these conditions is not met in a situation of paradigm comparison. As to the first condition, translatability, he seems to think there is hope; but Kuhn apparently believes the second condition, that the proponents of different paradigms must be talking about the same thing, is in some sense not met. According to Kuhn, one who holds a particular paradigm is "responding to a different world" from his or her colleague who holds another paradigm.[24] What Kuhn seems to mean by this is not that the two occupy "different worlds" in some naive, science fictional way, but that they have such a deeply different understanding of things that no mere dialogue across paradigms can possibly make headway, so different that the meaning of any apparently co-experienced event is different for each.[25]

Some readers will find this line of thinking reminiscent of the tradition in linguistics often identified with Edward D. Sapir and Benjamin Lee Whorf. Sapir, for example, once held that "(t)he worlds in which different societies live are distinct worlds, not merely the same world with different labels attached."[26] Whorf's treatment of the concepts *time* and *matter* in Hopi and English emphasize the same premise as he concludes that these concepts "are not given in substantially the same form by experience to all men but depend upon the nature of the language or languages through the use of which they have been developed."[27] It is not clear to what degree Kuhn's view is similar to this approach, and we make no claims on that score, but recalling it may be helpful in this context.

Finally, one feature of Kuhn's 1970 postscript requires mention. There Kuhn replaces "paradigm" with "disciplinary matrix" and proceeds to distinguish its four "components": symbolic generalization, models, values, and exemplars.[28] Since Kuhn only calls the last component one that "paradigm" would be "entirely appropriate" for, those who would cite Kuhn's paradigm thesis as interchangeable with a thesis about models have some adjusting to do;[29] and at least some breadth has been taken out of the original Kuhnian thesis as well. Interestingly, Kuhn does remark in passing at what seems a crucial possibility for ameliorating the difficulties[30] about which he is so exercised:

Briefly put, what the participants in a communication breakdown can do is recognize each other as members of different language communities and then become translators. Taking the differences between their own intra- and inter-group discourse as itself a subject for study, they can first attempt to discover the terms and locutions that, used unproblematically within each community, are nevertheless foci of trouble for intergroup discussions... Having isolated such areas of difficulty in scientific communication, they can next resort to their shared everyday vocabularies in an effort further to elucidate their troubles. Each may, that is, try to discover what the other would see and say when presented with a response to which his own verbal response would be different.... Each will have learned to translate the other's theory and its consequences into his own language and simultaneously to describe in his language the world to which the theory applies.[31]

Basically, Kuhn here urges that advocates of different paradigms or disciplinary matrices should regard themselves as speaking different languages. Unfortunately, besides the fact that this suggestion is not unique, no tools are offered the would-be translators to begin the work. Indeed, the very nature of their work remains obscure based on Kuhn's remarks. One is therefore uncertain as to what Kuhn's recommendation comes to at this point.

Karl Popper has taken Kuhn to task for not taking translatability seriously enough, or regarding it as some unlikely ideal rather than readily achievable. Popper calls this alleged error "the myth of the framework":

> The central point is that a critical discussion and comparison of the various frameworks is always possible. It is just a dogma—a dangerous dogma—that the different frameworks are like mutually untranslatable languages. The fact is that even totally different languages (like English and Hopi, or Chinese) are not untranslatable, and that there are many Hopis or Chinese who have learnt to master English very well.[32]

In his reply to Popper, Kuhn takes a different approach to translatability than in his postscript. First, he shares the doubts of most recent philosophers that there is no prospect for a theory-neutral language that could be a medium of translation; and he reiterates his view that although the same signs may be used in two different scientific languages their "meanings or conditions of applicability" have subtle differences.[33] Kuhn accepts the "utility, indeed the importance, of the linguistic parallel," but holds that "the difficulties of learning a second language are different from and far less problematic than the difficulties of translation."[34] Even the most competent bilingual encounters grave difficulties balancing the demands of "accuracy and felicity of expression" in translation.[35] The compromises implicit in translation alter communication and, according to Kuhn's reading of Quine's indeterminacy thesis, there can never be a unique or perfect translation.[36]

However, Kuhn believes that translations would give "recourse" to scientists who hold "incommensurable theories" (or presumably, paradigms). On Kuhn's view this still falls short of theory-comparison, since there is no neutral language to set as the standard for comparison.[37] What recourse is available includes learning to translate "each other's theory into his own language and simultaneously to describe the world in which that theory or language applies."[38] Yet even with an achieved translation, which language one speaks is more a matter of "conversion" than of "choice" or "decision" in the absence of a theory-neutral language.[39] Short of an authentic theory-comparison, the consequences for the speaker of each language are characterized as "therapeutic," apparently limited to finding out how they differ rather than whose worldview merits adoption.[40]

From the translators' standpoint the therapeutic result is sufficient. 'They' are under no obligation to aid the speakers in deciding what language to adopt once and for all. By thus laying the basis for communication the mutual realization of similarities and differences can itself yield growth and revision in unanticipated regions of each world-picture.

We have been focusing upon Kuhn's notion of the paradigm in order to provide a background concerning prospects for translation of models; shortly Willard Quine's thesis of the indeterminacy of translation will be presented as a supplement to this effort. However, it is apparent that whatever we take Kuhn's paradigm or disciplinary matrix to be, it is not entirely the same as our broad and colorless working notion of a model, at least not after his 1970 postscript. Yet we are justified in using Kuhn's discussion as a reference point for our own concern to the extent that paradigms, however they are analyzed, also constitute a certain received way of interpreting a domain for scientific investigation. Further, by Kuhn's own account it seems that certain ways of talking are associated with each paradigm; recall his concern with translatability. To this extent, then, our interest in the sorts of problems the paradigm notion suggests is not misplaced, for many of these problems also infect our prospects for the translation of models, as we understand the term.

Our interest in the translation of models, though not inspired by Kuhn, also stems from questions of commensurability between models in science, particularly in the social sciences. However, as it presently stands, IT, which looked so convenient as an explanation of some recalcitrant differences among colleagues, shows an awkward side. Before we hesitated at the prospect that propositions of scientific knowledge and religious faith would be epistemologically collapsed; now we bristle at the even deeper underlying notion that there is no world apart from the way we happen to model it, and that this must be so if we conclude that models are incommensurable. But what sense can be made of this notion? Surely there is something "out there" quite apart from the way we happen to conceptualize it. Even the most rabid philosophical idealist admits this. Yet if there is something out there independent of our models, or some things all modelists can agree upon, perhaps it can be useful in "translating" from one model to another.

Another way of regarding IT retains and perhaps clarifies the force of incommensurability claims with lessened temptation to a radical idealism and does so by way of the notion of translation. Willard Quine's thesis of the indeterminacy of translation, though laden with difficulties we cannot entertain here, provides a sophisticated basis for IT in terms of translatability.[41]

Quine's most famous and most embattled rendering of the indeterminacy thesis begins with the figure of an intrepid field linguist visiting a primitive tribal society with which there has been no previous contact. Importantly, too, there are no linguistic connections, even indirectly, between this society and any known human society. This is therefore a challenge for a *radical* translation. A story is told that the would-be translator notices that the natives utter "gavagai" to each other whenever rabbits are present. Thus she enters into a tribalese-to-English manual of translation "'gavagai' means 'rabbit'." The rest of the translation manual will eventually be full of such translation hypotheses.

But how can the linguist be sure that the one-word native sentence "gavagai" does not "really mean" "undetached rabbit part" or "instantiation of rabbithood" or something else that could be intelligibly uttered whenever a rabbit is around? The point of the tale is that she has no such assurance, for any alteration in one line of the translation manual, in this case the "'gavagai' means 'rabbit'" line, could be brought into congruence with any possible native behavior around rabbits by suitable adjustments at other lines of the manual. And, at least *ex hypothesi*, behavioral evidence is the only evidence of "meaning" that she has. Furthermore, two translations from two different manuals of the same sentence in the native language could actually provide incompatible interpretations of the native sentence while both whole manuals of translation "fit" all behavioral evidence.

Notice that a Quinean translation manual is like our very general idea of a model in the respect that both specify a certain ontology. Just as competing models of mental illness leave us with ids or groups, for instance, competing translation manuals leave us with rabbits, undetached rabbit parts, or instantiations of rabbithood, among other things. But who among us linguists can say which ontology is *the* ontology of the native worldview, or *the* ontology of the model? Given Quine's indeterminacy thesis, each translation manual has an equal claim, for their plasticity knows no bounds.

Or does it? In point of fact real translation manuals are sacrificed for others. Yet often not, it seems, out of any fault of their own, but rather because we get tired of them, they are too circuitous a route to our ends, they are too expensive, they are unpopular, and in these respects and others their competitors look more attractive. These conclusions also fit with the earlier allegation of a Kuhnian IT that extra-systematic considerations influence our choice of model. But in this case we are considering which of various ways we should interpret the model; this is another, albeit related, question.

It would be helpful if we could bring Quine's indeterminacy thesis closer to home than idealized translation manuals in radical contexts, in order to make sure that its introduction aids IT in its destructive task of undermining prospects for translation between models. In particular, we want to move from a context of radical translation to a thesis relevant to translation under less thoroughly alien conditions. To this end the most direct route is an adaptation of Quine's remark.

> (I)f we recognize with Peirce that the meaning of a sentence turns purely on what would count as evidence for the theory, and if we recognize with Duhem that theoretical sentences have their evidence not as single sentences but only as larger blocks of theory, then the indeterminacy of translation of theoretical sentences is the natural conclusion.[42]

In other words, given disconfirming evidence for some theory T, which lists theoretical sentences $t_1, t_2, t_3 \ldots t_n$, we could, according to Quine, elect to adjust any sentence at all in light of the evidence, since no single sentence is "the" sentence which is false. Now suppose we wish to translate T into another language. In doing so we are free to translate each sentence as we wish, so long as the total effect of the translation explains and predicts the same set of empirical data as T before translation. That is why Quine concludes that we are again left with a thesis of translational indeterminacy.

Of course there are some important differences between the setting of Quine's example and our own project, especially since we are not operating in a context of radical translation. Further, we are not translating a theory expressed in one natural language into another language, but rather certain sentences couched in terms of a certain model into sentences couched in terms of another model, with both models expressed in the same natural language. Let us suppose that we are successful in our later claim that this still counts as a genuine case of translation, even though numerous syntactic and some semantic problems are thus avoided. Let us further suppose that the historical accidents that render some persons bilinguals with respect to some pairs of models do not eliminate indeterminacy in principle, since bilinguals are simply individuals who unconsciously hold translation manuals "in their heads".[43] In that case indeterminacy apparently still reigns since no particular sentence suggested by a model must be adjusted in order to bring the model in line with some new evidence, and so systematic comparison of one model with another is impossible, since, by a series of ingenious interpretative adjustments, they can always be made to account for the same evidence. In other words, the sentences suggested by the model can be interpreted in various ways that nonetheless each bring the whole model in line with the available data. Some of these interpretations may even make the models inconsistent with another.[44] Further, since theoretical models are still less systematically related sets of sentences than the theories *they* interpret, the room for random adjustment among sentences to empirical data must be at least as great. Now, since choice of a model's interpretation is indeterminate, the ground for measuring one model against another falls away, hence the incommensurability among models.

Clearly our aim in this project is not the resolution of the problems raised by Quine, nor is it even to certify these as genuine problems.[45] However, a reading of IT along Quine's lines does us the service of showing how closely related are questions of commensurability and the nature of translation. It is important that IT, even on a Quinean reading, need not deny that adequate translation from one mode of discourse to another can be performed, nor that it is commonly performed by competent translators. However it does require us to stipulate our use of "translation" and at least guidelines for knowing when we have adequate ones. That is, even if we give up trading with the idea of sameness of meaning in our accounts of translational activities, some activity bearing earmarks of our pre-systematic notions of translation can still go on. Regardless of the fact that traditional accounts of meaning and translation may in this way invite IT, translating itself does function with at least pragmatic criteria of the sort mentioned above for comparisons among candidate translations. Ironically, our ultimate reading of IT suggests that those adequate translations that humans have achieved, and surely there are some, have been arrived at without an unproblematic theory of meaning. Put another way, incommensurability, if it does infect relations among models, and translatability, if it exists as it seems to, may be compatible after all.

One reason that incommensurability and translatability may be compatible is that the former denies an independent reference point for comparison among models, but that is not the same as denying that there is anything at all apart from the models. Recall that in Quine's anthropological example there are such things as stimulus conditions for "gavagai" even though the meaning of that sentence remained indeterminate. Without commitment to Quine's behavioral theory of language, we can nonetheless use a related approach as the basis of one sort of translation strategy, one that takes advantage of the presence of certain shared "applicability conditions"[46] to assist in devising interpretations in the terms of another model. This strategy will be the complement of another that especially but not exclusively treats expressions apart from association with such conditions.

When we first addressed the matter of locating the philosophical difficulties in a proliferation of models of madness, we specified a weak interpretation A, that "the different models of madness sometimes disagree in some, but not all, questions of etiology, epidemiology, pathology, therapy and nosology." Now we can say of A that it errs by omission, for if IT is taken seriously, we have to admit the possibility that disagreements among models may not be simply locatable by experimentation or by observing the verbal behavior of the modelers. IT holds that disagreements among models are matters of interpretation of the models concerned, as are agreements, for that matter. So the point is to come up with the most plausible interpretation of each model, i.e., those interpretations that make the most sense of each modeler's verbal behavior from the translator's standpoint. This is exactly what the translator must do with the several translation manuals available, given Quine's indeterminacy thesis. The fact that translators do not ordinarily work in contexts of radical translation suppresses the "fact," on this view, that countless manuals are available. Like the translator of natural languages, the translator of model languages has some practical advantages over the radical translator in Quine's figure (though these may not eliminate the underlying indeterminacy), including the opportunity to become a bilingual, the existence of expressions that are cognate with those in known tongues, and especially a knowledge of the syntax of the object language. As translators and language-users we might not bury IT, but we do manage to co-exist with it for practical purposes.

The attitude of the translator in the field, impressed with the range of problems for translation posed by IT, is analogous to Israel Scheffler's suggestion[47] that, in the face of severe obstacles to a modern empiricist theory of truth, we regard the claims of sentences as *credible* at a given time rather than *certain* for all time.

That a sentence may be given up at a later time does not mean that its present claim upon us may be blithely disregarded. The idea that once a statement is acknowledged as theoretically revisable, it can carry no cognitive weight at all, is no more plausible than the suggestion that a man loses his vote as soon as it is seen that the rules make it possible for him to be outvoted.[48]

Similarly, that a certain translation is thought to be revisable because according to IT all translations are revisable without end, does not oblige the translator to abandon it in spite of its credibility given current conditions and information. In other words, pragmatic considerations such as historic acceptance of a current translation or its comparative simplicity with respect to another translation otherwise of equal merit count toward retention of our own credible translation.

Finally, we have tried to convey a somewhat "arms-length" attitude with regard both to Kuhnian and Quinean approaches to a thesis of incommensurability. Our purpose has been to provide as forceful and general a rendition of the supposed epistemological gulf between mental illness models as we could, because we want to avoid appearing facile in our treatment of problems of translation between the models. However, as our primary task is to guide translators wisely rather than discourage them entirely, our agnosticism toward a view that puts the very substance of translation at hazard is strategic rather than apologetic.

On Models

Before turning our attention to issues of translation *per se* some closer attention is due for the type of entity we propose to translate. In several fields recently, including the study of psychotherapy, discussions have taken place concerning the relation among various "models" that are taken as candidates for the direction of theorizing and practicing in the area. Indeed, it has become rather the received view that too many models spoil the product, that some one approach must, for various not always well-articulated reasons, become the standard for guidance of practitioners.[49] For example, what is regarded as the current "enormous turmoil in psychiatry" is alleged to have its origins in the pursuit of different "models of madness" which "may confuse professional goals" by offering "competing theories of disease, conflicting models of treatment, or inappropriate professional activities." Hence, it is concluded, a single model must be fixed upon for direction of continued work in the field.[50]

This apparently simple claim, while not obviously false, raises a thicket of further issues touching upon many disciplines. These include the nature of scientific models, the relation of models to one another, the differences between models and theories, the sense(s) in which models offer "competing theories," and the role(s) of models in psychiatry, among others. Even a cursory examination of these matters reveals that fixation upon a single model is a more subtle notion than it appears to be, and not necessarily commendable even were one sure what it means. This is not to deny that severe difficulties are at times created, for clinical contexts anyway, by the presence of different ways of representing the facts of a case or, we might as well say, by the presence of different sets of facts supposedly constituting the same case. But we must state carefully what the conceptual origins of these difficulties might be so that we can begin to see the prospects and limits for their practical amelioration.

As it stands the notion that a plurality of models generates actual problems for the conduct of psychiatry is uncertain in its implications. Here, for instance, are several conclusions one could draw from the argument mentioned above, each apparently amenable to observation.

1. The presence of different models of madness makes it difficult for students in psychopathology courses to answer diagnostic questions on examinations.
2. The presence of different models of madness makes it difficult for hospital administrators to design psychotherapeutic programs with confidence.
3. The presence of different models of madness makes it difficult for some specialists to be published in certain journals.
4. The presence of different models of madness sometimes makes it difficult for practitioners to agree on treatment strategies for their patients.
5. The presence of different models of madness sometimes makes it difficult for the nursing staff to pursue confidently or even consistently the therapeutic program set out by the physicians and psychologists.

The list could be expanded. The point is that the breadth of inferences we could draw from the above contentions is great, but that from a logical standpoint none of the inferences entails any of the others. That is, 5 could certainly be the case without it being true that 1, and vice versa. Certainly such relationships may be perceived to hold, and may even in fact hold, but this is not the same as saying that the argument *logically entails* these and numerous other conclusions we could formulate. Conversely, the existence of a plurality of mental illness models becomes a convenient scapegoat for all manner of shortcomings in the field. By the mere enumeration of plausible expectations in a multiply-modeled field we will never be able to determine exactly the force of the thesis that the turmoil in psychiatry stems from a plurality of models.

Two conclusions commend themselves if we decide that there are in fact several mental illness models and that harmful confusion results. One is that we ought to work toward the development of a single, received model by means of theoretical and experimental interaction among the several models. This could take the form of ramification of a single model of sufficiently liberal scope by the well-confirmed conclusions of others; or it could mean the joining of all models, or those considered accepted, into a single grand "meta-model."

Now we do not necessarily agree that either sort of bridge should be built among models, either several leading to a single model or one so prepossessive as to create a single land mass. Our doubts are not so much clinical as philosophical, having to do with the degree to which models are indeed discriminable and discrete parts of psychiatric theory and practice. However, whether or not we are eager volunteers for bridge building, we can pose a prior question: Since presumably each model purports to describe exhaustively all phenomena commonly described as instances of mental illnesses, or to be able to do so in principle, and each purports to be able to do so in its own terms, how can we tell how large the divides are among the models? If in some unrefined sense each model portrays a "world" of mental illness, how different are these worlds and how can we know that?

The matter becomes less puzzling if, assuming there are several discrete models, we take models as languages and attempt to translate between models. The untranslatable residue then constitutes the substantial differences between and among models, rather than the merely "semantic" or "political" differences. Certainly whether we are committed to a confederation of models under a single head of a union of all in one, or even if we prefer to permit each to continue to govern its own domain, the extent to which there are actual differences will be of interest.

We might elect to continue the independence of each model because we doubt they can be compared at all. In that case we could neither "reduce" all models to one nor design a grand model to embrace all, for we could not know when or if we had ever satisfied the aim of either project. Hence the idea of incomparability needs examination; for us it will turn out to be a formal problem relevant to the *theory* of translation, but not debarring construction of translations in practice. Both the two sorts of bridge-builder and the non-bridge-builder, then, have an interest in translation among models, if that can be achieved.

In these remarks we have indulged ourselves by letting slide loose talk of models and theories. In part this reflects the laxity current in popular speech, and in part the state of the art in identifying and distinguishing the kinds of concept-clusters in science. But some clearer accounting of the differences should at least be recorded, one which also serves to recognize our terminological handicaps.

If we take the received view in the philosophy of science, then basically a theory can be regarded as a set of systematically related sentences, including some sentences that describe relevant conditions, and others that express certain relevant laws as hypothetical generalizations. These condition- and law-statements are held to exhaust the kinds of sentences there are in a theory. They are also thought to be deductively related, at least in a fully articulated theory, and thus the conclusive sentence is deducible from these premises. The conclusion, of course, describes the phenomenon to be explained or predicted, and the sentences that logically imply the conclusion as a unit constitute the explanation and assert the prediction. The standard *deductive-nomological*[51] model for theory structure can be schematized:

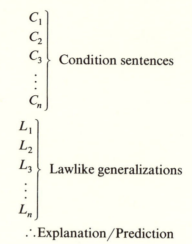

$$\left.\begin{array}{c} C_1 \\ C_2 \\ C_3 \\ \vdots \\ C_n \end{array}\right\} \text{ Condition sentences}$$

$$\left.\begin{array}{c} L_1 \\ L_2 \\ L_3 \\ \vdots \\ L_n \end{array}\right\} \text{ Lawlike generalizations}$$

$$\therefore \text{Explanation/Prediction}$$

There are, of course, important technical qualifications and problems in this view of theories; this view continues to undergo revision, but it will do for our discussion.

As to *models* of mental illness, it must be admitted that there has been little clarity in the literature concerning what kind of creatures they are, though this does not distinguish discussions of models of madness from those of other sorts. Nelson Goodman has noted succinctly that "model" in various kinds of discourse has come to mean "almost anything from a naked blonde to a quadratic equation."[52] Hence, we may do well to array a number of different sorts of models and define them as best we can, before settling on a working account of the way the term is used in contexts having to do with mental illness.[53]

In *formal logic* models are entities that satisfy axioms, such as the idealized points and lines in geometric diagrams; or they are the sequence of sets that correspond to each predicate letter, with the first set in the sequence comprising the objects that serve as the universe or range of values of the variables in the system. A *semiformal* or *mathematical* model is a theory containing the axioms of probability along with an interpretation of all or some of the nonlogical constants and variables of the theory into empirical observables. *Simplifying* models "distort" the original to make it more accessible to the student or lay-person, or are used in cases where the complexity of the original inhibits calculation. There are also *working* models or "analogues" which are objects structurally analogous or isomorphic to the original, such as the wind-tunnels or electronic models of nerve nets; they are employed where implications would otherwise be prohibitively difficult or even impossible to draw. *Theoretical* models are interpretations of a formal or semi-formal system from which statements about observables are deducible, such as a system of mechanical corpuscles being an interpretation of Newton's laws of motion.[54]

In the social sciences the use of the notion of a model, insofar as it is self-conscious, seems often to refer to a theory that is patterned after an existing one, such as general ethnography that utilizes concepts borrowed from a linguistic theory, say *component* or *deep structure*. On the other hand, the notion can also refer to the pre-existing theory on which another theory is "modeled."[55] In both these senses a model is a theory, while in the above senses a model is the range of entities *about* which its theory or theories speak.

Our problem is to come up with a working notion of a model that is adequate in accounting for the ways it is used in mental illness contexts and also general enough not to conflict with any more regimented usages. Prudence suggests that we take seriously the idea that models are at least interpretations of some sort, for this is a feature of all the better-defined senses of the word. To say that they are sets of entities that satisfy the axioms of a theory (its law-statements), is safe enough if we are careful to remember that many of the theories we use do not have as yet a readily determinable set of axioms. So far, then, models specify what kinds of things the theory is talking about.

Further, models make no assertions in themselves, for that is the job of theories, but they do effectively constrain what there is for us to talk about so long as we operate under the auspices of a particular model. To put matters more positively and in line with some versions of the theoretical models already mentioned, models are sets of predicates with an entrenched usage, and therefore familiarity, in a related area, or are the entities referred to by these predicates. Thus later we will speak sometimes of models "suggesting" statements or "leading us to disagree" with those who hold another model. Subsequent remarks concerning statements "from" a model or "in the language of" a model should be understood as elliptical for these more cautious but awkward locutions. We will also point out that models, although interpretations of a sort, are themselves open to interpretation in terms of the statements about observable phenomena or unobservable structures they could lead us to utter.

We will shrink from assuming that models are a kind of loose theory, as is often apparently assumed in the social sciences. Theories may "model" but they are not *qua* theories models, in our sense of the term, since the idea that models are assertive makes them so much like theories that any difference between them begins to vanish. We are better off sticking to the understanding that models suggest or lead to or inspire quasi-theoretical assertive statements quite apart from the condition- or law-statements that appear in any theory.

Still, we seem to be able to capture with this cautious approach what social scientists want to include as necessary to the notion of a model: The general sorts of things one is led to say in light of some posited entities or structures. We can thus think of models as heuristic devices that inspire us to say certain things that sound theoretical or to develop theories. The language of a model, then, is just the typical sorts of things or ordinary way of talking we are led to by adopting a particular model as our own.

As an example, the particle model of light leads us to utter statements about light particles, the wave model of light statements about light waves, and the wave-particle model statements about wavicles. Similarly, the medical model of madness suggests statements about biochemical compounds, the psychoanalytic model statements about ids, egos, and superegos, and so on. This convention also avoids the error frequently committed which suggests that models are exclusive in suggesting utterly different sorts of statement, for the bounds of "suggestibility" are psychological matters not specified by models themselves. Hence the psychoanalyst need not deny the intelligibility or the veracity of statements about biochemical compounds, nor the social modelist those about the ids.

It may seem that all this wrestling with the nature of models could easily be avoided if we settled for talking about theories of mental illness instead. But this would not be true to the literature that is our reference point, nor to the intentions, albeit often somewhat hazy ones, of those discussions. As a scientific community we still seem to lack a full-fledged theory of abnormal psychology that is as well-articulated as, say, some physical theories, replete with law-statements sufficiently accepted so as to permit application to condition-statements and deduction of consequences. Moreover, there are respectable epistemological grounds for opting for a contextual approach to a number of general pictures given diverse purposes, rather than incorporation of all models into one or all theories into a single model. After all, we have already seen that even unification of all theories into a single grand theory under a grand model, or of all models under a grand metamodel, still must be a certain sort of unification, one among countless ways of doing so.[56]

Notes

1. Joseph R. Royce, ed., *Toward Unification in Psychology* (Toronto: University of Toronto Press, 1970).

2. *Ibid.*, p. 157.

3. Nicholas Ch. Tatsis, "Translating Social Reality," photocopied paper.

4. *Ibid.*, p. 13.

5. Ronald Fieve, *Moodswing* (New York: William Morrow, 1975).

6. Tony Colletti, "Psychiatric Oppression and Class," *Win*, 15, No. 4 (August 1979): 5–31.

7. Miriam Siegler and Humphrey Osmond, *Models of Madness, Models of Medicine* (New York: Macmillan, 1974).

8. Dell Hymes, "Linguistic Method in Ethnography: Its Development in the United States," in Paul Garvin, ed., *Method and Theory in Linguistics* (New York: Mouton, 1970), pp. 251–253.

9. *Ibid.*, pp. 234–35.

10. *Ibid.*, p. 65.

11. Eugene A. Nida, *Toward a Science of Translating* (Leiden, Netherlands: B.J. Brill, 1964), p. 1; and George Steiner, *After Babel: Aspects of Language and Translation* (New York and London: Oxford University Press, 1975), p. 239–40.

12. Smith P. Bovie, "Translation as a Form of Criticism," in William Arrowsmith and Roger Shattuck, eds., *The Craft and Context of Translation* (Austin, Texas: University of Texas Press, 1961), p. 40.

13. Renato Poggioli, "The Added Artificer," in Reuben A. Brower, ed., *On Translation* (Cambridge, Massachusetts: Harvard University Press, 1959), p. 144.

14. Herbert Blumer, *Symbolic Interactionism* (Englewood Cliffs, New Jersey: Prentice-Hall, 1967).

15. Harold Garfinkel, *Studies in Ethnomethodology* (Englewood Cliffs, New Jersey: Prentice-Hall, 1967).

16. Peter Winch, *The Idea of a Social Science* (London: Routledge and Kegan Paul, 1958); and "Understanding a Primitive Society," *American Philosophical Quarterly* 1, (1964): 307–324.

17. Walter Benjamin, *Illuminations* (New York: Harcourt, Brace and World, 1968), p. 72.

18. Siegler and Osmond, *Models of Madness, Models of Medicine*, pp. 206–209.

19. T.S. Kuhn, *The Structure of Scientific Revolutions* (Chicago: University of Chicago Press, 1970). Kuhn himself uses the term "paradigm" in his more general discussion of the nature of scientific progress. However, this difference in terminology seems insignificant for at least two reasons. First, Kuhn defines paradigms as provident to scientists of "models from which spring particular coherent traditions of scientific research" (p. 10); second, it is stated that paradigms, like the understanding of models stated in the Preface above, are "object(s) for further articulation and specification under new or more stringent conditions" (p. 23). "Paradigm" and some of its theoretical baggage is dropped by Kuhn in his 1970 postscript. Margaret Masterman has claimed that Kuhn uses "paradigm" in not less than twenty-one different senses". See "The Nature of a Paradigm," in Imre Lakatos and Alan Musgrave, eds., *Criticism and the Growth of Knowledge* (London: Cambridge University Press, 1970), p. 61.

20. *Ibid.*, pp. 10–11.

21. *Ibid.*, pp. 35–39.

22. *Ibid.*, Chapters VI–VII. According to Kuhn paradigm choice is possible by balancing "values," such as the scope, simplicity, and fruitfulness of one paradigm against another, a common thesis in current philosophy of science. See Kuhn, "Objectivity, Value Judgment and Theory Choice," *The Essential Tension* (Chicago: University of Chicago Press, 1977).

23. For a further discussion of this topic in Kuhn see John Watkins, "Against 'Normal Science'," in Lakatos and Musgrave, eds., *Criticism and the Growth of Knowledge*, p. 36.

24. *Ibid.*, p. 111.

25. The reader of Kuhn's *Structure* is struck by some apparent wavering on the force of the notion that different paradigms determine different worlds. For example, Kuhn asserts that scientists don't quite undergo merely a "seeing as" Gestalt switch but rather "simply see" in a new way (Kuhn, 1970, p. 85); while on the other hand he refers to a falling stone that Aristotle and Galileo might see, as for one a change of state and for the other a change of process, thus apparently admitting some kind of "seeing as" phenomenon (p. 124). In the former case that "the world" is harder to make out than in the latter case, for "simply seeing" the *world* differently is more subtle than the straightforwardly psychological "seeing the world *as*."

26. Edward Sapir, "The Status of Linguistics as a Science," in Maurice Mandelbaum, ed., *Selected Writings of Edward Sapir* (Berkeley: University of California Press, 1949), p. 162.

27. Benjamin Lee Whorf, "The Relation of Habitual Thought and Behavior to Language," in John B. Carroll, ed., *Mind, Language and Reality* (Cambridge: MIT Press, 1956), p. 158. See also bearing on these matters Willard Van Orman Quine, "The Problem of Meaning in Linguistics," *From a Logical Point of View* (Cambridge: Harvard University Press, 1953), pp. 61–62.

28. Ibid., pp.181-187.

29. Furthermore, those who would be Kuhnians in order to situate philosophically the championing of a particular model of madness run the risk of undermining their own position when that model does become the dominant view, for then their own urgings of humility could be turned against them, given the relativity of paradigms, by the proponents of new, rival models.

30. Even our cautious characterizations of these matters do not hint at the complexities of these issues, which have inspired a minor industry. For a sampling of criticism of Kuhn's paradigm thesis see Israel Scheffler, "Vision and Revolution: A Postscript on Kuhn," *Philosophy of Science*, 39 (1972): 366–374; Dudley Shapere, "The Structure of Scientific Revolutions," *Philosophical Review* 73, (1964): 383–394; Dudley Shapere, "Meaning and Scientific Change," in Robert C. Colodney, ed., *Mind and Cosmos* (Pittsburgh: University of Pittsburgh Press, 1966); and Dudley Shapere, "The Paradigm Concept," *Science* 172, (1971). For his defense see Kuhn's "Reflections on My Critics," in Lakatos and Musgrave, eds., *Criticism and the Growth of Knowledge*. For a defense and extension of Kuhn see Wolfgang Stegmuller, *The Structure and Dynamics of Theories* (New York: Springer-Verlag, 1976).

31. Kuhn, *The Structure of Scientific Revolutions*, p. 202.

32. Karl Popper, "Normal Science and Its Dangers," in Lakatos and Musgrave, *Criticism and the Growth of Knowledge*, p. 56.

33. Kuhn, in Lakatos and Musgrave, eds., *Criticism and the Growth of Knowledge*, p. 267.

34. Why Kuhn thinks this is the case is not entirely clear. Certainly there are grave difficulties in explaining how one learns any language at all, let alone how one learns a second, and on the face of it this seems as complex a puzzle, albeit from another angle of concern as that of translation.

35. Kuhn, in Lakatos and Musgrave, eds., *Criticism and the Growth of Knowledge*, p. 267.

36. *Ibid.*, p. 268. Of course one need not be a Quinean to deny prospects for either unique of perfect translation, and in any case uniqueness and perfection are distinct characteristics.

37. *Ibid.*, p. 268.

38. *Ibid.*, p. 277.

39. *Ibid.*, pp. 276–277.

40. *Ibid.*, p. 276.

41. Willard V. Quine, *Word and Object* (Cambridge: MIT Press, 1960), Chapter II. There is a deliberate perversity to the examples Quine adduces on the way to building his thesis of translational indeterminacy. It seems that only under such extraordinary conditions can our attention be focused on some features of language that under ordinary conditions we could hardly detect. Further, in the discussion of the indeterminacy thesis that follows it is actually the indeterminacy (or inscrutability of *reference*) that is argued, though the essential problem underlying his more general claim concerning sentence-meaning is also given, and is expanded upon in subsequent remarks in the text.

42. Willard V. Quine, *Ontological Relativity and Other Essays* (New York: Columbia University Press, 1969), pp. 80–81.

43. *Ibid.*, p. 5.

44. During the discussion of Kuhn we noted that incommensurability does not even allow for logical incompatibility. Setting up incommensurability among models via Quine's indeterminacy thesis *does* involve the prospect of incompatibility, but not between models, which are incommensurable. Rather, the indeterminacy infects the interpretations of the models. Since any model can be interpreted in various, even contradictory ways, models are incommensurable. Indeterminacy thus infects the relation between the interpretations of a particular model, and incommensurability holds between two models as a result.

45. For one collection of discussions of the thesis of the indeterminacy of translation see Donald Davidson and Jaako Hintikka, eds., *Words and Objections* (Dordrecht: D. Reidel, 1969). Noam

Chomsky has criticized the thesis in several places, especially *Reflections on Language* (New York: Random House, 1975), and in Davidson and Hintikka, eds., *Words and Objections.*

46. Unlike Quine's "stimulus conditions" our applicability conditions are practical guides for translation, and not a complex of circumstances necessary for manifesting particular dispositions to verbal behavior, which for Quine are definitive of language.

47. Israel Scheffler, *Science and Subjectivity* (Indianapolis: Bobbs-Merrill, 1967).

48. *Ibid.*, p. 118.

49. Certainly much the same can be said of the natural sciences, in at least some cases, and of the humanities.

50. Paul F. Huston, "Forward", in Miriam Siegler and Humphrey Osmond, *Models of Madness, Models of Medicine* (New York: Macmillan, 1974).

51. See C.G. Hempel, "The Function of General Laws in History," *Aspects of Scientific Explanation* (New York: The Free Press, 1965).

52. Nelson Goodman, *Languages of Art* (Indianapolis: Bobbs-Merrill, 1968), p. 171.

53. We are grateful to Robert Feleppa for his comments concerning the following discussion.

54. See Mary Hesse, "Models and Analogies in Science," in Paul Edwards, ed., *The Encyclopedia of Philosophy*, Volume 5 (New York: Macmillan, 1967). See also articles by R.M. Campbell, B. Braithwaite, and M. Spector in Baruch A. Brody, ed., *Readings in the Philosophy of Science* (Englewood Cliffs, New Jersey: Prentice-Hall, 1970).

55. See Mridula Adenwada Durbin, "Linguistic Models in Anthropology," in Bernard J. Siegel, Alan R. Beals, Stephen A. Tyler, eds., *Annual Review of Anthropology, Volume* 1 (Palo Alto: Annual Reviews Inc., 1972).

56. See Nelson Goodman, "The Way the World Is," *Problems and Projects* (Indianapolis: Bobbs-Merrill, 1972). Certainly it would be desirable to have a more formal account of our working notion of models. To this end it could be appropriate to extend R.B. Braithwaite's and F.P. Ramsey's analysis of the status of theoretical concepts (*Scientific Explanation*, New York: Cambridge University Press, 1953). Thus, consider the status of an electron within the deductive system of contemporary physics, specified the following proposition:

> There is a property E (called "being an electron") which is such that certain higher-level propositions about this property E are true, and from these follow certain lowest-level propositions which are empirically testable.

"Nothing is asserted about the 'nature' of this property E," Braithwaite continues, "all that is asserted is that the property E exists, i.e. that there are instances of E, namely, electrons" (p. 79). Now, let us say that we are speaking instead of the theoretical *term* "electron", or to a symbol representing it. Then an answer to the question, "Do electrons really exist?" is answered indirectly by referring to the use of the symbol in the formal calculus of the system "from the bottom upwards" (p. 80). In this way, also, the meaning possibilities, so to speak, of the term are limited by fixing a range of its possible syntactical relations. To speak about a model is speak about these interpretations of the relevant symbol or term.

Much more needs to be said about the applicability of this approach to our own case; for one thing it is not clear that any or all theories of mental illness are or could be axiomitized as deductive systems, so it is not obvious that they can be modeled formally along the lines suggested. But this analysis at least describes how models could function for certain fully axiomitized theories both to specify certain theoretical terms and to constrain the ways one could use those terms under the auspices of that model. At least this analysis can give us a more rigorous idea of what could intelligently be meant when people talk about theoretical models, whether the term is used too loosely in some cases or not.

2

Basic Concerns and Techniques

From philosophical and sociological works on translation, and especially from discussions by natural language translators, we will adapt in this chapter some basic issues and tools for translating between models of madness. In some ways our arguments are nothing more than an elaboration of the prescripts that Etienne Dolet identified in the sixteenth century as crucial to any translation:[1]

1. The translator should have a perfect grasp of the content of the original text and goals of its author.
2. The translator must proceed from the sentence, not word for word, lest the integrity of the original be compromised.
3. The translator should rely upon forms of speech in common usage within the language into which he is translating, rather than import neologisms or rare words.
4. The translator will compose in a style that is both appealing to the audience in the new language and with a choice and order of words appropriate in tone to the original.
5. The translator must have a deep and equal knowledge of both of the languages.

Little can be added to the first of these admonitions, except to say that in translation of models quite as much as in natural language translation, the rule applies. A translator who does not admire and fully understand the work he or she is translating is likely to miss those finer points of thought and expression that make work significant. Good translators tend to read and reread the authors they translate and to respect and adopt their goals and ways of talking.[2]

The second dictum, which has received support in the philosophy of language from Frege to Davidson, will require a good deal of discussion, (which begins in the following section), because it defies an intuitive notion of what a translator between models would do. On first blush it seems perfectly reasonable that the translator should operate as a kind of concept lexicographer, preparing dictionaries for theorists of various schools, or bringing terms from one model to another.

Dolet's third and fourth points might seem unimportant for our purposes. After all, these are technical and, at least potentially scientific models, not poems or novels. What difference does writing style make for science? Such a view erroneously worships technical writing supposing that it convinces in ways radically different from other forms of presentation. Although it is true that the adequacy of a model depends primarily upon logic, insight, and valid observations, we shall see that style of presentation is not unimportant.

The fifth caveat reads like a platitude, but at the end of the chapter we will suggest that in the case of translations between models, bilingualism is of utmost importance and not a simple notion. On the one hand, it is not clear that anything like the knowledge of a "native" language is involved, and this raises the question of what language is to be used for translating models and whether a model's "language" can be taken on in a deep sense. On the other hand, we want to ask if there *should* be an emphasis on the original models, rather than the utilization of a meta-model.

Concept-by-Concept Translation

After momentary reflection upon our claims and goals thus far, anyone who has actually worked with or studied the disparate models of mental illness is likely to ask a question along the following lines. "How is it possible to translate a concept into a model that not only lacks the concept, but actively denies any place to that sort of concept? How, for instance, could a behaviorist model, which denies the existence of anything mental or actor-like, accommodate a concept like *Oedipus complex* from a psychoanalytic model?"

The query, while perceptive in ways we will discuss in the next sections, indicates a fundamental misunderstanding about translations. The focus upon concept translation is natural enough—common sense suggests that translation is the replacement of a word with an equivalent word—but that would preempt successful translation. Almost without exception,[3] translations fail that encourage a word-by-word or concept-by-concept matching. Although words or concepts are among the basic units with which the translator operates, translating them one after another in a string, or singly in a vacuum, will succeed as poorly as would the construction of an edifice brick by brick without a blueprint or cast. In a proper model or language, each concept or word performs specific tasks by way of its own composition and its location in a system of other units. This is recognized in even the most rudimentary machine translation programs, which entail combination patterns as well as dictionaries.

"The tendency to think of the meaning of a word, e.g., *apple, boy, dog,* or *sun*," Eugene Nida reminds us, "as apart from an actual communication event is fundamentally a mistake, for once we have isolated a word from its living context, we no longer possess the insight necessary to appreciate fully its real function."[4] Much as the occasion of a boss calling a worker *boy* is likely to translate into Russian differently than a father calling after his *boy*, the psychoanalyst's own *ego defense* against the suicide of his patient is likely to translate differently into labeling theory than is the suicide act itself, which is considered by the analyst to have been an *ego defense* for the patient. As we will discuss in Chapter 3, there is legitimate disagreement about whether the need for different host model sentences in these sorts of examples results from varied source referents or from varied source commitments. This is quite distinct from, but additional to, the general philosophical problem of the identity of a concept when removed from a system of related concepts. The point to be made now is that a translator does well to appreciate occasions and intentions within the language users' projects in attempting to move between models. To do so requires at the very least a concentration not upon concepts but upon concepts in use.

The fundamental lexical unit becomes the sentence. Source and host model concepts rarely "mean" the same or are equivalent in the sense that there are identical definitions for two separate concepts in two models, but concepts can function in similar ways. The smallest unit within which concepts function is the sentence, where the grammatical apparatus for statement-making is present. In more formal terms, the sentence is the first unit above the boundary between individual items and syntagmatically self-contained units (i.e., units that relate systematically to the full text), apart from some exceptional clauses that are syntagmatically self-contained.[5] From a linguistic point of view, a translator concentrates upon sentences because it is there that one can begin to uncover how and where concepts are used. One could think of the entire text in which the sentence appears and the unit of translation, but we choose this kind of sentence because it suggests the text.

Quine argues that identification of synonymy of terms is ambiguous across languages because we cannot know how to interpret responses to a term by a foreign speaker. On the other hand, Quine has at least some confidence in our ability to identify synonymy between sentences, and he does so on the behavioral grounds that synonymy of sentences, but not of terms, "turns on considerations of prompted assent, which transcend all cultural boundaries."[6] Nelson Goodman makes a similar point, but without the criterion of behavioral assent for verification, when he notes that synonymy means more than that two terms apply to the same objects. In addition, when other words are combined in the same ways with the two terms, the resulting strings should also apply to the same objects.[7]

Word synonymy is still more difficult to guarantee than Goodman's allusion suggests. Consider the terms "bachelor" and "unmarried man." Though they should apply to the same objects, this does not assure synonymy. Further if we combine them with other words in the same ways, even applicability may be lost, as in the pair "that fellow is a bachelor of arts" and "that fellow is an unmarried man of arts."

Translators are led away from word-by-word translation not only by issues related to synonymy in general, but by the specific type of synonymy they seek. Translators are judged poor if they imitate the original text in the host language, working to reach as close a copy as possible. Because translation requires the re-creation of a text in a space filled with different items than that of the original, actual copying is impossible. In one way or another the translator must confront the issue of what type of creation to develop, and traditionally "what moves the genuine translator is not a mimetic urge, but an elective affinity: the attraction of a content so appealing that he can identify it with a content of his own, thus enabling him to control the latter through a form which, though not inborn, is at least congenial to it."[8] The synonymy sought is of a special kind that has to do with bringing the sense of a message, or of the work done by a concept, from its place in the source language or model to its place in the host. By concentrating at the level of words one is likely to miss these aspects.[9]

In any kind of translation, then, there are good reasons to begin above the word level. Social science models include a number of characteristics that make word-for-word translation even more problematic than in natural language translation. For one, the models include many semantically exocentric phrases, or units in which meaning is not understood properly independently from the meanings of the parts or from their arrangements, but must be comprehended on the basis of larger relations.[10] For example, "Jack is exhibiting secondary deviation," within labeling theory means that he is in a second phase of his deviant career, a phase brought about by public recognition of his deviant behavior during the earlier phase. Within other models, if the expression were used at all it would most likely mean that Jack is exhibiting a major form of deviation and also a derivative form, such as alcoholism within psychosis. In natural languages exocentric phrases are the exception and are limited primarily to figures of speech ("beating around the bush"); and endocentric phrases, or those with internally deducible meanings, dominate ("his marriage is secondary to his work").

Another difference is in the world-making effected by social science theorizing. The received tradition in natural sciences has been to seek the most predictive and elegant law-like statements possible to describe or explain nature.[11] The social sciences have been variously praised and condemned during the century old, ongoing neo-positivist versus anti-positivist debates, for their inability or outright refusal to adopt wholly that sort of tradition.[12] We need not enter the muddy waters of the debate to observe that much model building within the social sciences consists in large part of alternative applied ontologies. Unlike the natural sciences, where a materialism and realism are taken for granted, in the social sciences, one finds models such as symbolic interactionism and ethnomethodology that tend to reject materialism and realism, sociobiology that accepts them, those such as Freudian and functionalist that call for a mixed ontology at various locations within the model, and those such as Marxist where materialism and realism mean something different than in the natural sciences.

Although we would not extend the argument to social science modeling generally, in the case of mental illness theorizing the alternative worlds that have been offered by disparate models prove utile, and we would wish to protect their fundamental diversity. Perhaps the best known and most controversial example of this utility has been the new visions of everything from art criticism to diplomacy made possible by Freudian world views. A cleaner case is the effect of Szaszian views of treatment of psychiatric patients, which contributes to stricter involuntary commitment laws in some localities and to concerns by mental health professionals with "problems in living." This is not to deny that natural scientific models also make for social change, as nuclear physics has demonstrated in so many ways, but they do so by changing the environment, rather than by adding diverse ways in which persons can view the natural world. In the natural sciences, diverse theories generally are not available, but rather there tends to be a single dominant paradigm,[13] or certainly a single ontology.

We are arguing in favor of the fundamental diversity between models of mental illness. Rejection of that argument is certainly reasonable, however, on grounds such as the impossibility that all of the models can be correct (or at least equally correct). A person who, on this ground or another, rejects the argument for pluralism, will likely find the task of translating between mental illness theories less rewarding, but will nevertheless need to pay attention to a difference from natural language translation: That ontological commitments in the models vary markedly and are consequential, though perhaps not all pairs of models are as "ontologically diverse" as other pairs. The divide is no less steep than that which Quine noted between our "object-positing kind of culture" and those native cultures in which occasions, symbols, or stimuli are primary.[14] To treat *Oedipus complex* by way of the overt behavior involved therein for purposes of translating to behaviorism may be a fundamental error, because one is allowing the host's ontology to override the source's ontology. (Throughout the book we will adopt the convention of referring to the model or language that will be translated as "source," and that into which the translation will be carried as "host.")

Thus it appears that even the sentence will not do as the unit of translation, for sentences often do not reveal the ontology of a model, just as they will not necessarily inform us whether we have an object-positing or type-positing culture ("This is a rabbit" may be uttered in either case). Confronted with these and related problems, Quine claimed that translations are indeterminate. Other authors have concluded that while in some ways indeterminate, translations may be more or less adequate, but that one cannot rely upon sentences any more than words as fundamental units in the development of adequate translations. Hölderlin and Walter Benjamin, quite separately, argued that because sentences are context-bound and closely tied to the full text, analysis on the basis of sentences must lead to an infinite regression (actually, an infinite progression). Rather, these authors insisted, the individual word is the unit of life that must be studied directly.[15]

To return to the word because the sentence suggests the whole text, or even the entire project of the author, is not the only way out in seeking the units of translatability. George Steiner in his elegant work, *After Babel*, defines translation as "the transfer from one designative coherence to another"[16] and suggests that in good translations the translator works from that coherence. "The meaning of a word or sentence is no single event or sharply defined network of events. It is a recreative selection made according to hunches or principles that are more or less informed, more or less astute and comprehensive. The illocutionary force of any past statement is diffused in a complex pragmatic field which surrounds the lexical core."[17] One must work between the larger context or project of the author and the immediate words and sentences within that context.

No single event or string of events reveal history, but the historian will study carefully only certain selected events or a series of events, at least in the conventional historical view. He chooses these events because they embody the elements of change that explain the movement of history; these critical events are the vehicles that carry us from one epoch or phase to another. In declarative and explanatory prose such as that of social science models, sentences carry the action. The parallel to critical events would appear to be *claim sentences*, which provide the movement from observations and analysis to the model as a totality.

A claim sentence is not a statement of an observation *per se*, nor of a fine point, but rather is a declaration or implication of the characteristic contentions of the model (or of a particular branch of the model) with regard to the issue at hand. "John's Oedipus complex is not revealed solely by his behaviors" is thus not a claim sentence as we are using the term, because it expresses the ground upon which claims are made rather than the claims themselves. "John exhibits Oedipal tendencies" also is not a claim sentence, but an observation sentence.[18]

An example of a claim sentence might be the following: "John is suffering from an Oedipus complex; he free associates a great deal of erotic content about possessing his mother, and that he wants to be rid of his father." Of course, a claim sentence need not concern a particular clinical case. A related claim sentence to the above might be: "Persons who suffer from an Oedipus complex free associate erotic content about possessing their mothers and being rid of their fathers." The phrasing of claim sentences in actual translations may not normally be as clean as in these examples, and two or three sentences may be required, but some requisite elements of claim sentences are revealed: key terms, declaration of a state of affairs deemed true, notice of observables (or theoreticals or dispositionals)[19] involved, and phrasing in the usual manner of the model.

As suggested above, no sentence, including a claim sentence, can be translated without considerations of the model or text as a coherent unity within which the sentence fits. But a proper claim sentence may serve as a syntagmatically self-contained unit that can be translated from one model to another. The better the claim sentence, the more adequate the translation is likely to be. For instance, in the above example *free association* of erotic *content* properly carries a Freudian way of thinking and talking without which we might oversimplify the phenomenon in question (e.g., as fully conscious) or misidentify its nature (e.g., as eroticism).

Even if we have identified claim sentences that we wish to translate, there are serious questions concerning recreation of that claim sentence in the host model. In addition to the questions of machinery for so doing, there remains a variant of the question with which we began this section. Now that we have cleared the ground of the fallacy of asking the question in concept-by-concept terms, the issue becomes: How is it possible to translate a claim sentence into a model that actively denies any place to that sort of claim? As things stand we have clarified the primary unit that must be brought from one model to another, but have not suggested how it is possible to make the conceptual transfer or translation.

Are Models Like Languages?

To back up, then, we must ask whether, or to what degree, we can talk about true translation between models. After all, translation takes places between languages, and we are proposing translation between models that are in the same natural languages. Are we not using "translation" merely metaphorically?

One response to this question is that in working with, say, "behaviorese," we are utilizing the English of everyday conversation, plus the technical terms of a behaviorist (e.g., reinforcement schedule), much as with "Durkheimian talk" we have everyday English plus technical sociological terms (e.g., anomie). Then behaviorese and Durkheimian talk are different languages even though they are part of English. Translating a model in behaviorese into Durkheimian would be quite analogous to translating from French to English.

From another point of view, we can suggest that standardly languages are distinguished from theories on the ground that a theory is a body of sentences asserted to be true, while a language is something else. For example, within current physical theory, "Neutrinos have mass," is asserted to be true; the sentence is "true in" physical theory because it is a part of physical theory. No sentences are "in" language the way they are parts of theories. No competent speaker of the language would on the basis of English competence alone be expected to assert the truth of that sentence. Of course, some sentences are necessarily true or necessarily false, earning their truth-value from their meaning or logical structure. "A bachelor is an unmarried man" is the familiar example of a sentence true, as is often said, by virtue of its meaning alone. "Bachelors are bachelors" and "Fred is and is not a bachelor" are examples of sentences that are, respectively, necessarily true and necessarily false. But it is the fact that the sentences in theories are asserted to be true by virtue of their membership in a body of sentences constituting a theory that ordinarily is taken to distinguish theories and languages. Like novels, theories are often in the English language but are not the English language.

Sometimes, though, we hear loose talk about "the language of physics" or "the language of psychology," and certainly there is something to be said for the notion that sciences, although their vital organs are theories, from an institutional standpoint have a language of their own. This could mean only that scientists speak in a jargonized dialect, on one extreme, or it could mean that the things they say *qua* scientists, when not uttering sentences strictly from their theories, are themselves parts of languages in the sense described above, on the other extreme. If we take the latter extreme seriously, it would mean that many of the sentences uttered by a physicist speaking "physicalese," for example, lack a known or believed truth-value in exactly the same sense that many sentences in natural languages lack a known or believed truth-value; and further that truth-value is only known or believed when physicalese is supplemented by a physical theory, just as "Fred is a bachelor" is known or believed to be either true or false only when supplemented by our relevant observations about Fred and the "laws" of bachelorhood, e.g., if Fred is still an unmarried man, then he is a bachelor.

Richard Rudner[20] has argued that reading Kuhn and Quine in light of one another undermines the distinction à la Carnap between theories as sets of assertions within a language and languages as structures determined by formation rules and semantical rules of interpretation. For Quine ontological commitment hinges upon what entities we permit our variables of quantification to range over, and not names. An example is n in $(\exists n)$ (n is a neurosis). Here n is the variable and "neurosis" is the name. So languages come, on the matter of reference, to be only trivially distinguished from theories; while for Kuhn meanings of terms in theories are theory-laden, so theories come to be construed as languages insofar as they determine the meanings of their terms. Surely models, which would apparently lie somewhere between theories and languages in the old view, could with at least as much force be argued to be quite indistinguishable from languages.

To take another angle, while it is true that our models are not natural languages, they bear at least two relevant similarities to natural languages. One of these also follows from the Rudnerian analysis cited above of the implications of Kuhn and Quine. But, setting incommensurability aside, the point is that expressions appearing in a technical mode of discourse, such as that of a social science model, have significance relative to that mode of discourse, just as is the case for natural languages. One cannot suppose that the appearance of replicas of the same expressions in two different modes of discourse entails the sameness of meaning of those replicas. This can be illustrated by means of semantic contrasts between elements of replicas of the same expressions in two different modes of discourse. For example, the pair of expressions "physician-patient" seems to have a greater semantic contrast in the medical model than in the social model, which is immediately suggestive of a difference in meaning.

T. Tymoczko[21] claims that semanticists must know ("have a theory of") the social environment of a society just as much as they must know the physical environment; otherwise the semantic contrast for a particular language community in the pair "capitalist-worker" will go unconsidered. Similarly, "physician-patient" carries a semantic contrast that depends upon the model in which it appears. Thus although certain replicas of certain expressions appear across models, their significance is often different; and if we admit fully the implications of IT, their significance must always be different.

A second similarity between models and languages is simply that neither admits of exact translation. That not even human natural languages can be translated with perfect equivalence is a proposition worth emphasising since it eliminates one apparent difference between models and languages. Edward L. Keenan[22] has argued against the notion that there can be exact translation from any one human language to another because "there are numerous areas of human activity which are not shared across certain language groups." If this is the case for natural languages, then we ought not to be surprised that perfect translatability between model-languages is out of the question. In this context Keenan's remark is especially telling since our models themselves represent areas of activity that are not universally shared by practitioners of the discipline.

Nida makes a similar point[23] in a discussion of the sometimes alleged impossibility of any translation at all. In these cases "absolute" rather than "relative equivalence" is unrealistically expected: "If one is to insist that translation must involve no loss of information whatsoever, then obviously not only translating but all communication is impossible ... loss of information is part of any communication process." As for natural languages, then, loss of some material in translating among models in unavoidable owing to what might be generally called cultural differences between the speakers.

Again, those who embrace IT must find whatever seemingly adequate translations that we do possess as unexplicated so far. Hence for them the notion of a fair translation is quite as mysterious as that of a perfect translation. As a matter of fact, however, we do have some expectations, however naive they may seem to the incommensurabilist, as to what criteria an adequate translation should meet. These should apply to the translation of models as well as that of natural languages (as considered in detail in the following chapter).

Stephen David Ross[24] has suggested three general ways of construing translation. They help us to see how certain criteria of adequacy for translation are related to our conception of this activity. First, we might see translation as a series of implicit assertions about assertions, so that we expect a claim in one language to be "equivalent" or "faithful to" a claim in another language. Second, we might regard translations as certifiable by their authors, the way a map-maker certifies that the map is a fair, accurate, or even exact copy. Third, we might take a clue from representational art: "Translation, then, might be a faithful representation of an author's work in the medium of another language, to be evaluated in terms of its faithfulness—but not its faithfulness alone."[25]

The first account is too strong, for we cannot always expect the same claim to be made in a different language, even if we knew how to construe "same claim," because there are languages in which certain complex technical claims cannot be made.[26] For a similar reason ambitions for copies, and certainly for exact copies, are bound to be frustrated, because not all equivalences will be sustained in any attempt at translation. Those equivalences that are sustained attest to the interpretive aspect of translation. "It follows that, with respect to the range of equivalences involved, every translation is an interpretation."[27] Ross concludes that translations are "active judgements," seeking by means of action to attain certain effects, requiring adjustment according to the circumstances.[28] In turn these adjustments will include conveying as efficiently as possible the different connotations of replicas (homonymous expressions) into the language of another model.

There is some warrant, then, in thinking of strategies of translation in the case of the relations among social science models in much the same way as we think of them in the case of relations among languages. If this line of thinking is on the right track, then the received disease-oriented psychiatric viewpoint, for example, is a language of its own expressed in medical modelese. But a further problem intrudes, for the medical model does seem to postulate entities in a way that natural languages do not. The "world" of the medical model is a world of diseases, lesions, bacteria, among other things, while the "world" of the English language includes both horses and unicorns. To put it another way, a speaker of medical modelese would have no hesitation to quantify existentially over any of the purported entities commonly named in that language, while a speaker of English would bristle at quantifying existentially over such things as unicorns.

This way of distinguishing between languages and models is subtle and important but does not strike us as conclusive. Were there such things as *rendezvous* in the "world" of English before that term became an accepted part of the vocabulary of an English speaker? One could dismiss this example as simply a matter of a novel, and somewhat exotic, connotation for "an arranged meeting", but one could hold with equal reasonableness that an arrangement to meet and a rendezvous do not come to quite the same thing. Such arguments seem to us to be futile, though one need not be a Whorfian to suppose that what counts as the world for a particular language community is altered, however minutely, by the introduction of a new expression into the language. From this standpoint models do not differ essentially from languages in terms of whether they do or do not give us ways to express what we think there is. Both do, but models do so in a more obvious way, which is important given their role in inquiry.

Yet another difference, also problematic for us, may be emerging here. Certainly a competent speaker of English could intelligibly deny that there are horses; could a competent speaker of medical modelese deny that there are bacteria? Our answer would have to be that he could, but that having the model at hand and living in the community of scientists cooperating under the auspices of that model he would tend not to do so; just as an English speaker would tend not to deny that there are horses. The extent to which such remarks tend not to be made by the members of a certain model- or natural language-community is perhaps greater in the former than in the latter, which again testifies to the fact that models more explicitly constrain our talk about what there is than do natural languages. On the other hand, that one could deny such received notions about the model-world and yet be speaking the model-language testifies to a point of similarity between model-languages and natural languages.

Key Features of Languages and of Models

The comparison to natural language translation needs to be further specified, however, in terms of the traditional concerns of translators. Much of the activity in translations between natural languages is directed at answering the question: "Where they say X, what do we say."[29] To answer this usually requires that we ascertain three types of equivalence: lexical, syntactical, and intentional.[30] Elements such as words, sentences, and paragraphs are deemed lexically equivalent when a bilingual dictionary associates them one-to-one (e.g., in an English-Spanish dictionary, *cat* and *el gato*). Syntactical equivalence consists of replacing the grammar of the source sentences or larger units with parallel host grammars. The operation often depends upon understood or explicit conversion tables for conjugation, modification, combination, and other grammatical processes.

Identifying lexical and syntactical equivalence turns out to be uncomplicated only in a few cases of natural language translation. One basic difficulty is the frequency of one-to-many, rather than one-to-one correspondence of lexical terms between languages. Another is ambiguity in the uses of grammars. Steiner offers an example of the latter:

> The study of Shakespeare's grammar is itself a wide field. In the late plays, he seems to develop a syntactic shorthand; the normal sentence structure is under

intense dramatic stress. Often argument and feeling crowd ahead of ordinary grammatical connections or subordinations. The effects—*Coriolanus* is especially rich in examples—are theatrical in the valid sense. We hear discourse in a condition of heightened action. The words "ache at us" with an immediacy, with an internalized coherence which come before the attenuated, often wasteful conventions of 'proper' public speech. But coherence is not the same as that of common grammar. At two points in Posthumus's diatribe (lines 19 and 28) ordinary sequences and relations seem to break down. Thus some editors would read "All faults that may be named, that hell knows." Others prefer to keep the Folio text, judging Posthumus's lapses into incoherence to be a deliberate dramatic means. So nauseating is the image of Iachimo's easy sexual triumph, that Posthumus loses the thread of his discourse; in his enraged mind as in his syntax, Iachimo and Imogen are momentarily entangled.[31]

The third step is even less amenable to completion on the basis of clear and simple procedures. At the level of intent a good translator means to capture the style, purpose, and place of the original. "The main task of the 'complete reader'," Steiner says, "is to establish, so far as he is able, the full intentional quality of Posthumus's monologue, first within the play, secondly in what is known of Shakespearean and Elizabethan dramatic conventions, and, most difficult of all, within the large context of early seventeenth-century speech-habits."[32]

Translation is commonly defined as the production of close natural equivalents in a host language of the meaning and style of messages from a source language.[33] In an important respect, this task would seem to be more easily accomplished between social scientific models than between natural languages. After all model translation takes place within a single natural language, and so the problems of syntax are seemingly obviated by the common grammar of the two models. Lexical equivalence for most units would be assured, since many words and sentences are used in the same (everyday) senses by most all of the models. Only technical uses would provide difficulty. Even equivalent intent is promised at the fundamental level. All of the authors intend to be accurate, explanatory, within the broad conventions of twentieth century speech habits, and so forth. The sorts of problems that Posthumus poses do not, for the most part, seem to exist for our project.

Unfortunately, these advantages turn out to be almost trivial, because translation between models is only secondarily a search for equivalence. Sometimes a contribution of the translator is to show that models in the social sciences are saying the same things in different ways. For example, Donald Campbell has suggested that behaviorist and intentionalist models end up with some striking empirical convergences, which they couch in disparate phrases. Behaviorists talk of dispositions to respond to the world in certain ways, while intentionalists talk of dispositions to view the world in certain ways, but their predictions of task or verbal behaviors in given situations often agree. Campbell shows, for instance, the translatability of a claim from intentionalist models, that hostile persons project their view of the world onto others by seeing them as hostile. When translated into stimulus-response models, the claim is that other persons serve as stimuli generalized as hostile, such that habits develop and transfer in the manner of hostile response tendencies to the representative stimuli of particular other persons.

A good rule for the translator of models might be to search first for equivalence or similarity between models. Commonly, however, the translator finds no equivalence and little or no similarity. Many sentences in natural languages are equivalent—for example, "My son is six," and, "Mon fils a six ans"—because the languages attend to similar objects and relations, and in similar ways. In other cases equivalence is ambiguous. Is the French *aimer* the English *to like* or is it *to love*? In more difficult cases, one language will recognize and name an entity or claim while the other will not. Well known examples include the numerous types of snow in Eskimo languages when compared to other languages, and differences in the number of primary colors recognized in various vocabularies (even between those that are in many ways closely related, such as Russian and German). One need not be a Whorfian or a radicalized Wittgensteinian, in order to recognize that natural languages express and help to maintain varied experiences of worlds. This is a major reason why translation is an art of re-creation as well as an applied science of linguistics.

Two languages are separate systems of two nonidentical worlds and hence the range of meaning or possible normal connotations of a unit in one will never coincide precisely with that of a unit in the other. In the case of social science models the concepts and claims are not only different by way of historical "accident," but are deliberately so. They mean to attend to objects and processes in separate ways, often to attend to separate objects and processes.

The question, "Where Model One say X what does Model Two say?" is typically answered with "Nothing," or, "Nothing of the sort." Perhaps what should be asked is, "To what extent does Model One say the same thing as Model Two when One says X and Two says Y?" The best we can hope for as translators is that these answeres are not the only or complete stories, and that we can bring about an answer of the sort, "Model Two could say Y about A, but its authors do not know that it can." The behaviorist says that he has nothing resembling complexes, especially nothing as peculiar as an Oedipus complex, and yet the translator might identify outcomes of reinforcement schedules that do not involve any mind-units but do involve the required patterns of ongoing child-parent relations. If it is important to the Freudian (for more than only ideological reasons) that Oedipus complex always entails mind-units, equivalent translations into behaviorism are probably impossible, but it does not suggest that *no* translation of any kind is possible.

Rather, the discussion thus far suggests that features of social science models that must be considered in translating are not the same as those in natural language translation. On the one hand, most of the lexical and syntactical units are already in conventional equivalence because the models are written in the same natural language or have already been translated into a common natural language. On the other hand, equally fundamental features differ between models. These include ontological commitments, epistemological commitments, and style.[34] By ontological commitments is meant the types of objects and relations posited (mind-matter, diachronic-synchronic, causal-interactional, etc.). By epistemological commitments is meant the ways of knowing posited (*verstehen*, case study, experimental, etc.).

Style is, as usual, less easily defined than are the other features, but is quite important in translating between models. There are parallels to the stylistic differences Steiner notes interlingually in British society.

> The privileged speak to the world at large as they do to themselves, in a conspicuous consumption of syllables, clauses, prepositions, concomitant with their economic resources and the spacious quarters they inhabit ... . Watch the feigned responsiveness, menace, and non-information in a landlord's dialogue with his tenant or in the morning banter of a tally-clerk and lorry-driver. Observe the murderous undertones of apparently urbane, shared speech between mistress and maids in Genet's *Les Bonnes*.[35]

Or observe the angry young man style of the labeling and Left models compared to the coolly objective talk of neurological or biochemical models, and again one finds that the way of talking does much of the communicating. "Upper middle class women enjoy the boutiquing of psychiatry and engage in private therapy," writes an author for a special issue of *Win* magazine on mental health, "they are labeled neurotic, and it is considered in vogue. Lower class women are commonly diagnosed as schizophrenic, incarcerated in state hospitals, administered electro-convulsive treatment (shock therapy) and tranquilized into a stupor."[36] The authors of a behavioral neurology volume sound different:

> The idea that brain damage might allow full expression of a gene for schizophrenia can be invoked to explain the high incidence of neurologic and electroencephalographic abnormalities seen in schizophrenic patients. Available data suggests that there might be an autosomal dominant gene for schizophrenia, as there is for petit mal epilepsy, whose penetrance varies with the age of the individual and whose expressivity is in large part determined by the presence of acquired brain damage and by other genes which influence personality, adaptability, and other brain function.[37]

The strategy of the first author is to startle us into belief by bringing two worlds together ("tranquilized into a stupor"). The technique of the second author is to "expert" us into belief by bringing two worlds together (schizophrenia and petit mal epilepsy). Unfortunately, we cannot work our way out of the seductions by bracketing the styles and sticking to the proffered evidence. The first author has poignant examples, but one cannot tell if they are representative, and the second has a series of several impressive studies, but with small samples and disparate diagnostic protocols, and one does not know if the patterns really compare to epilepsy, since none of the studies looked both at schizophrenia and epilepsy.

In some cases one has even less opportunity to clear away the style with the hope of retaining some sort of purified claims. For instance, Freud takes the willing reader on a journey through his queries, spatially separating and yet stylistically integrating cases with claims. Too often readers have confused reststops along the way with destinations, taking the conclusion of a case history to be a generalizing law, considering a thinking-through of a key concept to be a final pronouncement, or concluding that if a case can be analyzed in a different way than by Freud, there is something amiss. Freud's claims must be derived from the body of his thought, and in this way his work contrasts with medical model styles, in which the reader is deposited as efficiently as possible at a clear conclusion. Compare this to Edwin and Willa Muir's distinction between German and English.

> The German language is supposed to be not unlike English, and word for word there are many resemblances. *Ein Glas Bier* can be recognized by an Englishman without translation. Yet a German paragraph is quite unlike an English paragraph; even a German sentence is unlike an English one. At its source the thought which flows into either is differently controlled and directed. From its first word a classical German sentence is purposively controlled until the verbs come down at the end of it to clinch the statement; one cannot be sure of the meaning, however one may guess, until these verbs are reached. The English statement has not this control; it cannot wait, or does not choose to wait, for the end of the sentence to convey its meaning. It runs on discursively, perhaps qualifying or changing its meaning, and uses verbs as they come in what seems to the English their natural order. To construct an English sentence is not unlike stringing beads one after the other.[38]

Having introduced the importance, but also the complications of style, let us set aside consideration of stylistic features of models until we have discussed strategies for working with the features of ontological and epistemological commitments. Our basic task is to accomplish translation despite differences in the models, and in the cases of differences in ontological and epistemological commitments, there are diagrammatic procedures employed by everyday language translators that we may adapt to our needs.

Diagramming Claim Sentences

In natural language translations some mapping procedures have been developed to assist in the transfer of lexical and syntactical items. Probably only a few translators work out the maps or diagrams explicitly but theorists of translation, and machine translators, have demonstrated the utility in some cases of developing these on paper.

J.C. Catford notes for instance, that *brother* from English and *cho* from Burushaski do not "mean the same" though they would frequently be used as replacement items for one another in translations.[39] These lexical items are from language cultures that attend to the ontic landscape, in this case to family items and gender, in different ways. *Brother* concerns the sex of the person being labeled and the sibling relation, while *cho* concerns the sibling relation and the sex of the speaker. The relationship of the English and Burushaski lexical items are tabulated by Catford in Figure 1 (with + indicating male, − indicating female).

By use of this figure translators avoid inflicting their own linguistic culture on the language being translated. When a male Burushin talks about his brother and uses *cho*, and then his sister uses *yas* in talking about the same person, who is also *her* brother, the English translator wants to take care not to confuse *yas* and *cho* for synonyms. To avoid the mistake requires something like Figure 2.

A table of this sort might be developed directly, for the specific lexical item in question, or it might be a second step in the translation process. One might first construct tables for the semantic field more generally at issue. Thus, if one wanted to translate family terms, he might begin by developing a table for these relations in each language culture. Such a table has been worked out by Nida[40] to describe English language culture:

a. Sex (s): male (s_1) and female (s_2).
b. Generation (G): two generations above ego (g_1), one generation above ego (g_2), ego's own generation (g_3), one generation below ego (g_4), two generations below ego (g_5).
c. Lineality may be described in three degrees: (l_1), in which the persons involved are direct ancestors or descendants of ego, and (l_2) (colineals) and (l_3) (ablineals), representing two successive degreees of less direct lineality.

English	Situation		Burushaski
	Speaker	Sibling	
brother	+	+	cho
	−	+	
sister	+	−	yas
	−	−	cho

Figure 1

	I_1		I_2		I_3	
	s_1	s_2	s_1	s_2	s_1	s_2
g_1	grandfather	grandmother	uncle	aunt	cousin	
g_2	father	mother				
g_3	ego		brother	sister		
g_4	son	daughter	nephew	niece		
g_5	grandson	grandaughter				

Figure 2

By working out this kind of componential analysis of meaning, one is able to ascertain the critical relations utilized by the language culture in making distinctions, and in the process of constructing the table unsuspected features or distinctions come to be recognized as important. Nida[41] suggests four steps in preparation of such a table:

1. Determining the limits of a "closed corpus" of data, i.e., limiting the study to a well-defined set of words that have multidimensional relationships consisting of certain shared and contrasting features.
2. Defining the terms as precisely as possible, on the basis of the objects involved. For example, for the English kinship term *uncle* we would specify father's brother, mother's brother, father's father's brother, and mother's father's brother, etc.
3. Identifying the distinctive features that define the various contrasts in meaning, e.g., differences of generation, of sex, of lineality, etc.
4. Defining each terms by means of distinctive features. For example, father may be defined as first ascending generation, male, and lineal (i.e., direct line).

To use this sort of tabular material for bilingual translation one would, of course, construct a similar table for the second language culture. The necessary column and row headings for any table of a subsection (e.g., *brother*) become apparent, and construction of translation instruments such as Figure 2 would be straightforward. In cases where there is no overlap, the translator is helped by shared folk wisdom, ("old wives' tales"), and everyday speech.

In translation of models, this sort of componential table would be constructed with different units in mind, as our discussion has suggested. Of course the boundaries of the cells are "fuzzier" than they appear to be; even the more obvious ones originate in translator's choice. Usually one would expect to map out a claim sentence as the primary unit. Since we seldom find lexical equivalence between models, it might be more confusing than insightful to construct tables for single terms. In some cases one might wish to do so as a first step, however, to identify the general places in the semantic fields in which to turn for translating. Recall, for instance, our sample claim sentence: "John is suffering from an Oedipus complex; he free associates a great deal of erotic content about possessing his mother, and that he wants to be rid of his father." The translator might prepare tables much like Figure 2 regarding *father* and *mother* in, say, Freudian and behaviorist models. If developed with care, they could reveal that in Freudian models, but not in behaviorist, one finds not only generational relations to ego (e.g., grandparents as two generations above ego) but also generations of parenthood. In some cases, the Freudian wants to say that an offspring wishes to possess what might be called a diachronic rather than synchronic mother; or put another way, he wishes to possess the mother of his childhood. So we may have in the Freudian model an additional feature to add to our tables.

If translators wish to map out other parts of lexical units from the claim sentence, however, such as *complex*, *free associates*, or *content*, they will require tools other than the componential table. This kind of table is applicable only to series of terms that have shared and contrasting features,[42] and is useful to the translator mostly to identify locations of such items in language or model systems. If one seeks the mapping of a term that is not part of a clear subsystem of related terms, a diagram of semantic structure is the appropriate translator's tool.

Figure 3 is such a diagram by Nida.[43] In parentheses are indicated the points of departure in meaning within the semantic structure. Parts of speech are noted by N for noun and V for verb.

Nida recommends four steps in developing this sort of diagram: "1) list all the possible meanings of a word, 2) group these by setting up ambiguous contexts for the most inclusive to the least inclusive classes, 3) determine the manner in which such ambiguities are resolved, and 4) apply satisfactory labels to the points of diversion."[44]

The result is, of course, a kind of "tree diagram" and as such allows one to build upon pieces of information when complete information is lacking. For example, if we know that we have a non-object rule, and we know nothing else, we can intelligently investigate the possibility that we are dealing with controlling-governing-managing, since these are the most direct meanings. Then we could begin to search for redirecting elements, such as evidence that a judicial rather than an executive dimension is present, to determine whether we are correct in our concluded meaning within a given usage.

This efficient use of the diagram is possible because the diagram is constructed on the basis of the observed use of the language relative to the item, rather than upon some idealized notion of how the language "should" be used,

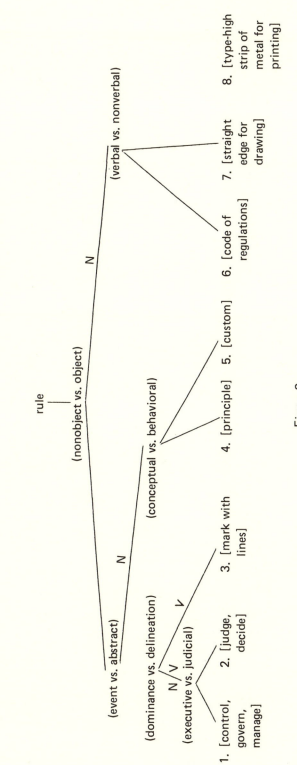

rule

(nonobject vs. object)

(event vs. abstract)

N

N

(dominance vs. delineation)

(conceptual vs. behavioral)

(verbal vs. nonverbal)

(executive vs. judicial)

N/V

V

1. [control, govern, manage]

2. [judge, decide]

3. [mark with lines]

4. [principle]

5. [custom]

6. [code of regulations]

7. [straight edge for drawing]

8. [type-high strip of metal for printing]

Figure 3

or something related to the material nature of objects or relations referred to by the term. This characteristic is especially important for applications to translations among social science models, because here it is necessary to emphasize the ways in which theorists "make" or "work with" referents. A Freudian and a behaviorist looking at the same clinical interview with a patient are likely to say different things about what they saw. In part this is because they attend to different aspects of the situation, and in part it is because the Freudian and behaviorist are involved in different social scientific projects. But unlike some natural science situations, the issue is not easily resolved on the basis of agreed upon arbitrating relations with the referent. If two natural scientists disagree about the color of an object, they can decide upon a measuring spectroscope whose readings they will both accept in deciding who was correct, though disputes about measurement are also possible. The objective physical aspects of color are the only aspects with which the scientists need concern themselves, and if they can agree in identifying the instrument that best provides that sort of data, the primary agreement can be reached and is fortuitous. In social sciences the situation is often quite different, if for no more sophisticated reason than that widely received instruments on the order of a spectroscope do not exist for purposes of arbitration. One cannot attach a machine to a person during a clinical interview and obtain data that either the behaviorist or the Freudian deems very significant about most of the issues involved in their disparate reports. Thus, one must rely upon the nature of their reports *per se* to work between theories. At the level of arbitration of conflicting claims, the process is twofold: To determine what, if anything, would count as evidence for or against the claim for each modeler; and agreement about empirical tests. Agreement about the internal coherence of the modelers' sets of claims could be added, to make a threefold process. All three operations can occur only after translation has been completed in some fashion, so that modelers know what in common is discussed by them in conflicting ways. As we have been suggesting, however, in other cases the issue is not arbitration of conflicting claims, but rather concerns unrecognized or currently unaccepted possibilities for theories to utilize one another's insights. As an aid in ascertaining such possibilities, any semantic diagram must be faithful to the language or model-world as it exists within a given theory, rather than as one might think that it should be, on the basis of an external logic or an analysis of the referents. Otherwise one is not aiding in communication (i.e., not translating) but is dictating or instructing in theory development.

In translation between models the semantic diagram *per se* is of limited use, however, as we hinted above. The reasons are easy to identify: Lexical equivalence is rarely available or sought; a single term in a single model rarely takes a wide variety of meanings; and concept-by-concept translation is ill-advised. In general for purposes of translation we do not require anything like an exhaustive description of meaning, but only clues to aid the translator in correct anticipation of verbal behavior or the sense of the message of native speakers. On the other hand, adaptations of the semantic diagram offer great promise as aids in model translating.

A claim sentence may be "unpacked" by means of these diagrams. Through a semantic diagram one can map out what is at issue within the claim and thereby identify what needs to be carried over to the host model. In constructing a claim diagram one undertakes approximately the same moves as noted above for construction of the semantic diagram of a term. First, as many meanings of the claim as practicable are listed. In our example, one looks closely at Freudian theory and discovers, for instance, that there are various ways John could be said to be suffering: habitually or somatically, behaviorally or mentally, as an actor or as a non-acting person, consciously or unconsciously, and so forth. Second, a hierarchy is developed, again by degree of inclusiveness, but in this case not as markedly as in Figure 3. Thus, would *actor and not-actor* or *conscious and unconscious* go higher in the diagram? Probably the question is unanswerable on the basis of relations within Freudian theory, although in other cases, the issue is clearer. The conscious-unconscious division is more inclusive (higher) than, say, a division in kinds of suffering of a complex (e.g., habitually versus somatically). In the Freudian view forms of suffering are either conscious or unconscious, and one would never claim the reverse, that the conscious or unconscious are forms of suffering.

In the final step, the translator identifies connections between units, by asking of the model which sorts of affiliations it permits and which it excludes. One might ask, for instance, whether in Freudian theory a person can be both unconscious and an actor with regard to a complex. In short, the diagram of part of a model seeks the possible meanings of the unit being diagrammed, as does the semantic diagram, but departs from the latter by building not terminal meanings (the bottom of Figure 3) but rather combination possibilities within the diagram. One reads the diagram of a model across, the semantic diagram down (shortly to be described in detail).

When an entire claim is diagrammed, the result is inevitably more elaborate than Figure 4. One major reason is that claims, or parts of claims, do not fall into neat binary oppositions. While they do involve the two major branching

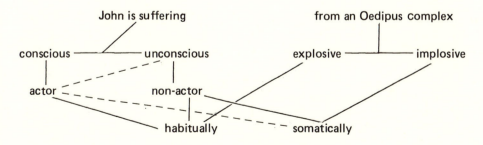

Figure 4

markers found in Figure 3—dichotomies (e.g., nonobject verus object) and behavioral contrasts (e.g., executive verus judicial)[45]—the models entail many other divisions as well. In Freudian theory, for example, one can imagine dividing markers such as ontological contrast (e.g., physical-mental), severity differences (e.g., neurotic-psychotic), consciousness distinctions (e.g., conscious-unconscious), or directionality (e.g., implosive-explosive). The branching may often go in more than two "shoots" or directions. Freudian theory recognizes, for instance, a physical-mental-conjoined split with regard to the nature of mental illness.

The absence of a clean binary structure makes machine diagramming more difficult, of course, and also contributes to the irregularity of the resulting shape of the tree. A major contributor to this effect is the absence of an either/or structure in places. In Figure 3, this either/or branching at the level of object versus nonobject obviates the possibility that one can have both an event and a verbal rule. In the case of model diagrams, and surely also in some cases of natural language diagrams, the branching may carry one far less determinately from the top of the tree to the bottom. Instead, there are often various, though a finite number of, paths one can take around the diagram. Consider the fragment of a diagram, Figure 4, which is a hypothetical example of the way that part of a claim sentence diagram might look. (For actual diagrams of claim sentences see Chapter 6).

This diagram reads somewhat differently than that of Figure 3, but aids in a similar way in translation. Among the obvious differences is the inclusion of broken and unbroken lines, the former representing firm connections in the model, the latter representing unlikely but not excluded connections. The pairs of markers (e.g., conscious-unconscious) are not deemed dichotomous, because one can claim within Freudian theory that with regard to Oedipus complex a person's actions are partly conscious and partly unconscious, or both habitual and somatic.

Whereas a semantic diagram of a term assists the translator by revealing routes to particular terminal meanings, claim sentence diagrams specify the possible elaborated versions of the claim, or what might be called claim meanings. Several such claim meanings may be derived from the diagram fragment presented as Figure 4. For instance we see that the claim may mean that (1) John is suffering consciously, and thus as an actor, and thus perhaps somatically, or (2) John is suffering unconsciously, and thus not as an actor, and thus either habitually or somatically; and if habitually then explosively; and if somatically, them implosively. The translator has available various shortcuts, then, in his task of translating between models. For instance, if he knows that in the text John's situation is regarded as deriving from the unconscious rather than the conscious, then if the condition is described as habitual, the complex manifests itself explosively (other-directed), whereas if the condition is described as somatic the manifestations are implosive (self-directed). This knowledge will give him clues about where or now to place the claim in the host model.

To follow through on the example, suppose the translator determines through these sorts of markers within the diagram, the claim that John is *unconscious*, *habitual*, and *explosive*. The translator then seeks in the host model (e.g., behaviorism) those ways of talking and thinking that attend roughly the same phenomena or events. The translator might work first with the ways in which behaviorism discusses habits, since there is a common element between the models. He would seek those ways of talking or types of habits that best resemble the Freudian's version in the source text. Next he might identify specific possibilities in behaviorism for talking about what Freudians call the unconscious, even though behaviorism denies mind units. It may be discovered that this element of translation is thereby unproblematic, because everything is unconscious within the behaviorist model. Or there may be "response dispositions," "conditioned responses," or such that behaviorists say entail the inability of subjects to identify that they are emitting patterned behavior. In searching for such units the translator must remain faithful to the source model's other distinctions, such as between instinct and acquired, and so would avoid those units in the host language that confound the distinction. In this case, an unconscious complex is something acquired, and hence any item from behaviorism that entails instincts will be unacceptable for use as a translation. Finally and probably least problematically, the translator searches for a way to describe in behaviorism that the complex is explosive rather than implosive. Probably all that would be needed is a clause in the final claim sentence in the host model such as "behaviors towards others."

The utility of the diagram will be judged by how well it facilitates such working across the largerly epistemological and ontological differences between models. Inclusion-exclusion and ordering rules for construction of diagrams depend upon the uses to which the diagram must be put. A Vermont map-maker decides whether to plot forests or to plot trees on bases such as whether the map is to be used for identifying places to camp in Vermont or for summarizing the potential lumber yield in the state. Similarly, the model translator decides which elements to include in a claim sentence diagram on the basis of what he considers to be needed in making a particular translation. If he includes *explosion-implosion*, it is because that feature of the model appears to be of some importance.

On what grounds does the translator decide that an element is important? We may preview Chapters 3–5 to note that construction of such diagrams, or of lexical tables, depends upon either or both of two bases. For some translators, who we will call extensionalists, units for the diagram are selected on the basis of referent: representations of actual objects or properties of objects to which the models apply. For other translators, who we call essentialists, units are chosen on the basis of the fundamental nature of the models themselves. Both types of translators may end up selecting *explosive-implosive*, for instance, but for extensionalists the choice is made on the ground that the models apply to this feature of the world, while for essentialists it is based upon this item bearing an important relationship to the fundamental units with which the models are constructed.

In either case, for a diagram to be useful for translation it must somehow relate to both the source *and* the host models. Although any diagram of a claim sentence will be constructed primarily on the basis of the nature of the source model within which it exists, it must do so with one eye to the host model.

Bilingual Translators

Much of the translation process consists in the translator searching through the host language or model for items akin to those he is bringing from the source. This may be aided by the use of dictionaries, or by construction of diagrams of what appear to be similar sorts of claims in the host model. The translator can then compare the diagrams to determine the points of overlap or parallel. In so doing the translator must think to himself about the possibilities and problems, and he must do so within some manner of talking. Should he conduct his translations within the language of the source or that of the host?

In the scholarly literature about natural language translation the problem is sometimes addressed as if there were no decision to be made: The translator thinks primarily in his own native language. The translator's native language is the host language in most cases, and the major aim of the translation is to present foreign material adequately in one's own language. In any case, one is destined to use one's native language as the metalanguage, because that way of thinking is the most natural.

Some theorists of translation argue, however, that the scales need not be tipped in the direction of either of the languages involved, because the translator may become fully bilingual.[46] The argument here is that the ideal translator would be equally comfortable and familiar with both languages and able to think in both almost simultaneously and continuously during the translation process. It is recognized that this goal is reached only in the very rare case of a translator who has long operated on a daily basis in both language systems (e.g., by living in a family where members speak both languages on all occasions). Most often translators are persons who have spoken one primary language throughout their lives but have learned another language.

In translation between models the situation differs. All model languages are acquired, and usually through intentional learning rather than "naturally" from daily usage. Some persons do devote themselves rather fully to one model, and that way of thinking and talking becomes almost inherent, as illustrated by the psychoanalyst who discusses her husband's ego defenses in everyday discourse with him. A thoroughbred psychoanalyst of this sort who decided to become a translator between psychoanalysis and another model would probably have quite as much difficulty becoming bilingual as would an adult speaker of English in learning to translate French and English fiction. For other translators between models, however, and including the present authors, no model is like a native tongue, because they do not customarily work from one theoretical school or hold a special dedication to a single school. The very motive for these translators to do their work may be their lack of devotion to a single model, or their broad appreciation for several models. Ironically, such bilingual translators may be in either the optimal or the most disadvantaged position for conducting translations between models. On the positive side, they need not be more at home in, nor committed to, one model over another. On the negative side, neither way of talking is "natural" to them, and so there is potentially alienation twice over, as against a natural language translator who learned anew one of the languages with which he works.

Luther once remarked that a false Christian or a nonbeliever would be unable to render a faithful translation of the Bible. No doubt it is as bad to be devoted to the text in an improper or ideological way as to be uninvolved with it. Our suggestion, as imprecise as it must be, is that the best translators of models will be those persons who become well educated about, and advocates for, *both* of the models with which they are working. In this way they avoid membership in the majority that Quine describes when he contends that "most talk of meaning requires tacit reference to a home language in much the way that talk of truth involves tacit reference to one's own system of the world, the best that one can muster at the time."[47] Where there is no home language but instead an equal involvement in both of the languages, no home exists for tacit referencing (though perhaps two homes may exist).

The truly bilingual translator is also in a better position to avoid the related difficulty of maintaining an appropriate tension between the texts. Much as one wants a Shakespeare play to be as fully artistic in the French translation as in the English original, one wants a claim from labeling theory to be as fully significant in the medical model translation as in the labeling theory original. A goal in translating models, as much as in translating natural languages, is to enrich the host with accomplishments of the source without in the process destroying or minimizing these accomplishments. To reproduce this significance the translator must protect the *labelingness* of the claim even while finding a way to talk naturally about the issue in medical model language. The tension arises between the polar risks of fitting into the host model in an artificially neat and domesticated manner something which that model did not (and probably would not) produce on its own, versus emphasizing the foreign nature of the source claim and thereby creating barriers to its acceptance within the host model.[48] We rightly suspect of compromise an English translation of a French novel if the street names in Paris have been changed to those of London; on the same grounds we question a translation of labeling theory into the medical model if schizophrenia is no longer an individual exhibiting behaviors and others responding to these behaviors but has become an illness or syndrome that the individual "has." On the other hand, we feel distant or antagonistic to an English translation in which districts carry only their French names, because we do not know whether the characters of the novel are in the suburbs or in a place like our own Piccadilly. A medical model reader feels similarly toward a translation from labeling theory in which schizophrenia is constantly referred to as "secondary deviance."

Maintenance of the proper tension between affinity and distinctiveness among models is accomplished by the translator's movement back and forth between the models, attempting to think within both as nearly simultaneously as possible. To do so one must avoid the commonsense notion that a translator works solely in the source-to-host direction. Rather, the host language is brought to the source quite regularly as well. Of necessity, when one identifies a sentence in the host that appears to be the proper way of putting a sentence from the source, one must then compare back to the source to check this hypothesis.

Some authors argue, however, for a more profound sense in which host-to-source movements might occur. Rudolf Pannwitz[49] has suggested that translations suffer when their goal is to turn the source language into the host language, because they thereby revere the host language more than the source. The translator errs in protecting the state of the host language instead of allowing it to be expanded or otherwise changed. The point is not that one should play freely with either language in order to translate, but rather that the source should receive as much of the change that inevitably results from translation as the host. In a balanced translation both the source and host can be enriched, and both should sacrifice equally their nonessential idioms.

Part of the translator's task is to re-create in the host language a clear version of the source material. In so doing it may be necessary to make the source clearer than it stood prior to translation. Analysts of translation have noted a number of cases—Kierkegaard, Hegel, Ibsen, Kazantzakis—in which the full voice and impact of a writer were uncovered by translation. One is reminded also of the effects in Germany of Norman Kemp Smith's translation of Kant's *Critique of Pure Reason*. Students there, although native speakers of German, have been known to use the English translation in order to escape some unnecessary stylistic elements of the original that interfere with usage of the text.

In some cases, it is only in light of a popular translation that the work is considered profound by speakers of its original language. For example, Faulkner's popularity in America increased radically after his critical acclaim in France, and commentators here talked about him in new ways. Other cases have been suggested where the original is changed fairly radically by the translation, with the result that the version in the second language fits the culture in which that language is spoken but still retains the key message and other characteristics of the original. Lin Shu's translations of Dickens into Chinese have been described in such terms. In Shu's version the talkativeness and overstatement of Dickens disappear, but the humor remains within the new, more sedate and frugal style.[50]

One can imagine similar beneficial changes in the case of source models we propose be translated. In the course of translating most any of the models of madness a careful translator can hardly avoid clarifying these models. This is in part due to the vagaries and underdevelopment for which the models are so often criticized. More fundamentally, the translator is compelled to specify clearly what is being said within the models in order to search for matching units between models. We can also imagine that a claim will be more deeply received by those working in its original model, in light of the results of translation. If a translated claim proves productive, or produces unexpected empirical or theoretical consequences in a host model, its significance might be better appreciated by persons working in the original model.

Reservations About Meta-models

Bilingual translation of claims is not the only way out of the problem of finding a language or model within which to conduct translations. An alternative approach is by means of a meta-model, or a model that would encompass the models being translated, by including in the extensions of its predicates all entities in the extensions of the predicates of all other models, perhaps. In this strategy the translator, who might then be better termed an interpreter, utilizes the meta-model as the language and way of thinking regarding the regular models, or uses the models to build a meta-model.

Arguments for the meta-model approach are significant. None of the extant theories in the behavioral sciences are complete or fully adequate; otherwise we would not need translation. A meta-model could operate as arbiter and integrator. By not moving to a meta-model we perpetuate the contrary claims of the various models.

A related argument for meta-models is the unification of science position. This approach to the problem of proliferating models points out the utility of each in its own context, denies that there is any necessary incompatibility among the models, and urges that each gives us part of the elephant, as in that hackneyed tale about the blindfolded men, each of whom touches a different part of the elephant and so describes it differently. On such a view we should rather encourage continued conferences of a multidisciplinary nature and establish clinical teams of individuals representing various perspectives, in order to iron out differences in practice and assist the process of developing a unified theory. The American psychiatrist Adolf Meyer, for example, advanced a "pluralistic objectivism" that regarded each of the specialized perspectives in the science of man, from the biochemical to the social psychological, as contributors to a fuller picture since all are functional in the explanatory process though they are diverse.[51]

Before commenting directly upon this sort of systematic pluralism, we should note that by no means do we object to the pursuit of interdisciplinarity;

on the contrary, scholarly and scientific disciplines unfortunately become hardened into administrative categories that often do not serve inquiry. However, the unifier needs first to distinguish between a set of *disciplines*, physiology, psychology, etc., and a set of *ideologies* within each of those disciplines and often cutting between them. It is one thing to hold that each of the disciplines gives us its own accurate picture of the universe; it is quite another to make such a claim on behalf of a number of ideological "isms." And it is often difficult to tell when we have one or the other, as in the case of psychoanalysis or some behavioral theories of personality.

More generally, though, the quest for unification of models into a grand meta-model is suspect in that it seems to presuppose that a single particular form of unity is possible, or even desirable. The story of the elephant assumes that there is an elephant "out there" just waiting to be fully characterized if we would only conjoin our perspectives. The suggestion that our models of mental illness should be wedded into a meta-model creates strange bedfellows at best; and the product of a union of medical modelists, social modelists, Szaszians, psychoanalysts, behaviorists, and the rest would be more like a duck-billed platypus than a dignified elephant. Unlike some physical sciences, there are not overlapping findings that are generally accepted as impressive evidence for the natural possibility of unification. In the physical sciences evolutionary and quantum theories have been extended profitably in a variety of disciplines, over seemingly disparate problems. In the social sciences the candidates for meta-models or tools to build such models have never been received without good arguments against them. The most recent candidate has been sociobiology, which apparently has upset at least as many social scientists as it has excited.

Admittedly, the form of the big picture generated by a meta-model would depend on the criterion used for joining some models in particular ways under certain contexts. If, as was the case for Meyer, our criterion if functionalistic, then we have already selected a certain picture rather than a variety of others that would have been produced if some other criterion for combination had been chosen, such as maximizing the models' collective utility in policy planning or efficiency for framing them into grant proposals. If we do not assume an objective elephant apart from our selected mode of unification, the limits to the form of that creature are the limits of our criteria of combination, but nothing else.

This form of the objection to investing too much confidence in the prospect of a single grand meta-model is pragmatic: Different modes of unification will give different pictures, but no one mode will give "the whole picture" because that cannot be said to exist apart from our chosen form of combination. A further meta-level for the forms of combination would be subject to the same prospect of multiple modes of unification, and so on *ad nauseum*. But this is only an informal version of the problem with the meta-model proposal: The meta-model is itself subject to whatever incommensurability infects the relations among the models, as alleged by IT. That is, each sentence of the meta-model could, it appears, be adjusted in various ways that bring the meta-model into line with the "data" constituted by the set of models, just as each of the models could be brought into line with available evidence in various ways. These possible theories of the meta-models could even be logically inconsistent with one another and still each constitute adequate expressions of the relation between the meta-model and the several models. Choice of a meta-model is therefore determined by which criterion of unification we prefer, an obvious circularity; while the meta-models themselves are incommensurable insofar as IT applies to the interpretations of meta-models as well as of the models themselves.

Meta-models are no way out of the radical problem alleged by IT concerning the proliferation of models, since then we have to deal with both the proliferation and incommensurability of meta-models. As we do not suppose that a particular mode of translation under either of our translation strategies will turn out to be an end-all, the illusion infecting the notion that there is some unique meta-model does not represent a hazard for us. Rather, with translation there is some hope that the claims originating in one model can be discussed or empirically validated in others. The kinds of translation we propose need not sacrifice the integrity or "turf" of any of the models nor require their proponents to think in ways they are unwilling or unable.

At the same time, translation may accomplish some of what is hoped for meta-models. Models may be filled in and otherwise made more adequate by inclusion of findings from other models, even when that inclusion is in the host model's own idiom. Translation also offers the possibility that contrary or contradictory claims will be mediated through empirical research. Moves toward unification may even result if modelers examine one another's claims and discover that there are appealing grounds for unified theory.

The Principle of Charity

Before plunging into our specific techniques for translation, one additional prescript should be noted. Like any serious translator the translator of models adopts Neil L. Wilson's[52] "principle of charity": "We select as designatum that individual which will make the largest possible number of ... statements true", compatible with empirical constraints. In other words, we do not assume that the advocate of a particular model has any false beliefs, or utters any false assertions, even though to the advocate of a rival model many of those beliefs and assertions are unintelligible or false. We assume that the claims of the modelist *qua* modelist are true, for our job is not to refute scientific views but rather to interpret them as efficiently as possible in the terms of another model. The translator of a natural language would be remiss not to translate a claim from a source language into the target language in such a way as to render the claim reasonable to a speaker of the target language. Instead, the translator takes the most plausible interpretation of the source claim, one which does not knowingly distort the intent of the native speaker but gives it its most reasonable expression, and puts it in the most sympathetic terms of the target language that remains legitimate for conveying the source claim.

The translators attempt to do what the modelers themselves cannot (and often would not want to do). They take claims that are well accepted in one model and put them in the mode of discourse of another model. They do so with the hope that now that they are written in terms that the host modeler understands and accepts that the host modeler will take them seriously, even if in so doing they are eventually rejected on grounds of empirical inadequacy, incompatibility with other well accepted findings, or for other reasons.

Notes

1. Nida, *Toward a Science of Translating*, pp. 15–16; and Steiner, *After Babel*, p. 262.

2. Justin O'Brien, "From French to English", in Brower, ed., *On Translation*. By this first rule we do not commit ourselves to achieving an objective grasp of meaning.

3. There are, of course, materials that can be so translated, for example, lists of common items (One: A dog, Two: A cat = Uno: Un perro, Dos: Un gato). Some technical works in the material sciences have also been translated between natural languages in that way.

4. Nida, *Toward a Science of Translating*, p. 40.

5. J.C. Catford, *A Linguistic Theory of Translation* (London: Oxford University Press, 1965); Paul Garvin, "Some Linguistic Problems in Machine Translation," in Morris Halle et al., eds., *For Roman Jakobson* (The Hague: Mouton, 1956).

6. Willard V. Quine, "Meaning and Translation," in Brower, ed., *On Translation*, p. 154.

7. Nelson Goodman, "Meaning", *Problems and Projects* (New York: Hackett, 1972).

8. Poggioli, "The Added Artificer", p. 141.

9. Paul T. Manchester, "Verse Translation as an Interpretive Art," *Hispania* 34, p. 68.

10. Nida, *Toward a Science of Translating*, p. 95.

11. cf., Carl Hempel, *Philosophy of Natural Science* (Englewood Cliffs, New Jersey: Prentice-Hall, 1966).

12. Fred R. Dallmayr and Thomas A. McCarthy, *Understanding and Social Inquiry* (South Bend, Indiana: Notre Dame University Press, 1977).

13. Kuhn, *The Structure of Scientific Revolutions*.

14. Quine, "Meaning and Translation," p. 155

15. Steiner, *After Babel*, p. 329–333; Benjamin, *Illuminations*.

16. Steiner, *After Babel*, p. 205.

17. *Ibid.*, p. 136.

18. See Quine, *Word and Object*.

19. In the sense that Richard Rudner discusses in *Philosophy of Social Science* (Englewood Cliffs, New Jersey: Prentice-Hall, 1966).

20. Richard Rudner, "Show or Tell: Incoherence Among Symbol Systems," *Erkenntnis* 12, (1978): 129–151.

21. T. Tymoczko, "Translation and Meaning," in F. Geunthner and M. Geunthner-Reutter, eds., *Meaning and Translation* (New York: New York University Press, 1978), p. 36.

22. Edward L. Keenan, "Some Logical Problems in Translation," in Guenthner and Geunthner-Reutter, eds., *Meaning and Translation*, p. 174.

23. Nida, *Translation: Applications and Research*, p. 63.

24. Stephen David Ross, "Translation as Judgment," in Marilyn Gaddis Rose, ed., *Translation in the Humanities* (Binghamton: State University of New York at Binghamton Press, 1977), p. 5.

25. *Ibid.*, p. 6.

26. *Ibid.*, p. 12.

27. *Ibid.*, p. 9.

28. *Ibid.*, p. 12.

29. Stephen Turner, *Sociological Explanation as Translation* (New York: Cambridge University Press, 1980).

30. Steiner, *After Babel*, p. 5.

31. *Ibid.*

32. *Ibid.*

33. Eugene A. Nida, "Principles of Translation as Exemplified by Bible Translating," in Brower, *On Translation*, p. 19; Catford, *Linguistic Theory*, Chapter 2.

34. These features all concern intent, and thus, for the natural language translator our task may be seen simply as intralingual translation in which intent, but not syntax, is varied between texts.

35. Steiner, *After Babel*, pp. 34–35.

36. Colletti, "Psychiatric Oppression," p. 6.

37. Jonathan Pincus and Gary Tucker, *Behavioral Neurology* (New York: Oxford University Press, 1974), p. 90.

38. Edwin Muir and Willa Muir, "Translating from German," in Brower, ed., *On Translation*, pp. 94–95. Perhaps it is not surprising that the more physicalist medical models have grown up in Anglo-American languages, the more hermeneutic in German and French.

39. Catford, *Linguistic Theory* pp. 39–40.

40. Nida, *Toward a Science*, pp. 84–85. This technique is similar to Goodenough's componential analysis approach.

41. *Ibid.*, p. 83.

42. *Ibid.*, p. 87.

43. *Ibid.*, p. 110.

44. *Ibid.*, p. 113.

45. *Ibid.*, p. 111.

46. Steiner, *After Babel*; Nida, *Toward a Science*.

47. Quine, "Meaning and Translation," p. 171.

48. Steiner, *After Babel*, pp. 392–393.

49. Quoted in Benjamin, *Illuminations*, pp. 80–81.

50. Steiner, *After Babel*, p. 396; John Hollander, "Versions, Interpretations, and Performances," in Brower, ed., *On Translation*.

51. Adolf Meyer, *Psychology* (Toronto: Ryerson Press, 1957).

52. Neil Wilson, "Substance Without Substrata," *Review of Metaphysics* 12, (1959): 521–539.

3

Two Types of Translation

We have suggested thus far that translations between models in the social sciences are needed if theorists, researchers, and clinicians are to be able to communicate between their disparate theories and if intertheoretic cumulation of knowledge is to be encouraged. Yet recent work in the philosophy of language and the philosophy and sociology of science seems to undermine the potential for translation in anything like a traditional sense. The upshot of these apparent obstacles—such as the incommensurability thesis (IT) and other arguments against the possibility for adequate translations, and differences between models and languages—is not the rejection of translation but the need for a critical and humbled perspective on translation endeavors. The previous chapter proposed the sorts of units to be translated between models and a sense of the kinds of techniques to be employed. But which sorts of translations do our discussions thus far indicate?

Presystematically, when we think of translation we suppose the translated sentence means the same thing as the original sentence. If we are a bit more sophisticated, we expect slight variations due to cultural or grammatical differences between the two. But if two models meant the same thing in all of their particulars, there would be no need for translation of any kind, since they are already in the same natural languages. Generally, when we think of sentences as meaning the same thing in two languages or models, we think either of conveying the same sense or of talking about the same things. Indeed, in the case of a great translation we are impressed by the retention of the message in both of these respects.

Perhaps it is possible to let these intuitions guide us to formulation of more formal translation strategies. On the one hand, if our ambition is to work with the sense of a sentence from a model, we can consider the basic units within that model with which the various meanings are built. Here we turn to essentialist traditions in philosophy and the social sciences, where there have been discussions of procedures and problems in culling the defining characteristics from texts or other objects. As applied to translation these traditions encourage that movement from one model to another be founded upon conceptual units and arguments that are ineliminable from the models. Technical problems will center on the identification and location of those essential units, and determination of how claim sentences are derived from them.

On the other hand, if we wish to attend to those purported objects referred to by adequate translations, there are relevant guidelines in the philosophy of language, and especially in some recent work on the theory of reference. This approach seeks techniques for isolation of observable common referents for utterances from different languages. These referents, once identified, in turn provide grounds for determining the extent to which there is a common meaning in respect of shared reference. Difficulties will include devising an apparatus for presentation of hypothesized common referents to informants from each model to test the degree of mutual applicability of expressions from each model.

To work from these traditions—the essentialist and the referential—is not to embrace these perspectives in full, but rather to take advantage of their speculations on, and techniques for analyzing, differences in ways of representing human experience. Thus, from theories of reference we need not adopt the naive view that meaningful talk about the world is limited by the range of actual material objects; and from essentialist theories we need not accept reductionism nor the confounding of necessity and sufficiency.

Since talk about the referents of a term is, in logic, to talk about the extension of that term, we call the referential technique *extensional translation*. Since the concern with bases for a model considers primarily the necessary units within that model, we call that technique *essentialist translation*.

While we discuss the two strategies separately, and while they do attend to the models in quite different ways, there is no reason in an actual translation to limit oneself to one of the techniques. In fact efficient translations will normally be constituted of a negotiation of the two strategies. Extensional and essentialist translations are complementary. The fundamental projects and structure of a model will have great bearing on the objects attended and the ways they are attended. Referential utterances are raw material for the essentialist in his search for necessary components of the models.

Both kinds of translation are accomplished in three lengthy stages. The translator develops or identifies the claim sentence; the claim is diagrammed in the source and host models; and by way of overlap between these diagrams the translator recreates the claim in host model terms.

The first of these stages involves careful attention to the source text(s) and selection of a complete claim. In the previous chapter we proposed criteria for knowing when one has a claim sentence. More than that will not be said in the following chapters, since choice of a claim sentence will depend upon the reasons that a translation is being conducted, not upon the type of translation strategy being employed. Thus, if one seeks to bring some major insights from behaviorist to psychoanalytic theory, it will not matter for the choice of claim sentence whether one is an extensionalist or essentialist, but rather which of the eligible claims one finds illuminating. The remaining steps will vary considerably between essentialist and extentionalist techniques.

Working with Two Translation Strategies

Nida[1] points out an aspect of the utile relation between our translation strategies when he notes that identity of semantic structures may be too much to count on in establishing conditions for successful translation. However, ordinarily there can be "substantial agreement on the pragmatic level," that of "referential function." Although our translators do not hold any particular theory of meaning, essentialist and extensional guidelines do point them in the direction of seeking analyzable units of similar concern on the one hand and partial referential equivalence on the other. Concerning the latter, Nida further states that "this dependence on referential function means that one must look to the nonlinguistic world for many of the answers to problems of translation equivalence." In the extensional strategy relevant features of the nonlinguistic world are ordinarily depictions of purported things or events. Through their manipulation referential agreement may be secured and confirmed, as Nida suggests, and clues may be garnered for the solution of problems of semantic equivalence by working with similar analyzed units, for which the essentialist strategy is particularly well-suited.

Furthermore, there is no conflict between the use of a certain strategy for translation and a translator's preference for a certain theory of meaning: "In actual practice, translators rarely if ever pursue their work as though they were guided by only one underlying theory."[2]

Translators with a penchant for a mentalistic theory of translation have no reason to feel they are "settling" if referential equivalence is evidently the efficient route to translation in a particular case, nor need a behaviorist be uncomfortable gleaning essential concepts for an hypothesized translation. Either strategy for the process of translation can be accounted for by means of a preferred theory of translation.

These remarks indicate how each translation strategy supplements the other for the translator in the field. Units derived from the essences of models can be checked against extensional equivalences, and the latter can be used as directives and inspirations for essentialist analyses leading to the discovery of similar units among models. There is no reason to think that this is a practical liberality, which is nevertheless philosophically repugnant. Take the example of that sort of philosophical anti-essentialist who, for whatever reasons, refuses to countenance talk of *properties* of objects as essential (necessary) or non-essential (contingent). That individual may still admit that some *predicates* do apply essentially to their objects, in which case there is an obvious rubric for combining essential and extensional translation strategies: take as the grounds of translatability just those essential representations in the secondary extension of an expression. These representations would be the ones that no competent speaker fails to assent to as applying to the object or theory it purports to represent. Any class of depictive representations essential in this sense to expressions in more than one mode of discourse is thus a class of representations essential to the extensions of all such expressions.

Problems for Extensional Translation

A number of specific problems with the two types of translation strategies will emerge as part of their detailed development in the next two chapters. Some difficulties pertinent to each can be considered in advance, beginning with one that encumbers translations generally.

All translations are implicitly on the defensive from what has been called the argument from semantic dissonance. As Steiner has noted, even "soixante-dix" and "seventy" have different semantic origins: "Nothing fully expressive, nothing which the Muses have touched can be carried over into another language without losing its savour and harmony."[3] The point is most often made with regard to poetry, but philosophic texts are by the nature of their subject matter uniquely susceptible to the least discriminable alterations in sense. But the argument is too strong, since the susceptibility of translation to the charge that it violates the unique circumstances of the original testifies only to the character of translation as one sort of speech act in a world that is not static. "Strictly speaking," Steiner writes in this vein, "no statement is completely repeatable (time has passed)."[4] Translation involves an extreme case of this generic feature of all actual speech, which hardly amounts to a ground for abandoning activities that offer countervailing benefits.

Still, this awareness should serve to heighten the attention of the translator to the context of utterance, particularly the extensionalist. J.C. Catford[5] provides an example of the way situational considerations affect prospective "transference of meaning" (Figure 5). In this case the situation has to do with the relation between the situation and a relevant question, but its particular nature should not distract from the general lesson of the import of context as established by non-linguistic or extra-linguistic features of situations as well. For the extensional translation strategy those features of the context that do or could fall within the extensions of key expressions are especially important.

In translation among models countless situational subtleties can be imagined to intrude, many of the pattern set forth in Catford's example: The way one contextual variable interacts with another constitutes the relation between hypothetically translatable expressions. This causes no difficulty, beyond deluding the translator that symmetry has been found, until that heretofore unencountered variable relation appears. Consider the simplified situation

	Question	Situation	English	Japanese	French
Did you? I did.	+	+	yes	hai	oui
Didn't you? I did.	−	+	yes	iie	si
Did you? I didn't.	+	−	no	iie	non
Didn't you? I didn't.	−	−	no	hai	non

Figure 5

described in Figure 6 wherein both Freudian and labeling modelers are represented as finding the expression "mentally ill" applicable to a hospitalized and delusional individual (though the reasons for this attribution differ widely for each). But this is not the case for the labeling modeler if the individual, though delusional, is not hospitalized. For the labeling modeler the individual is a deviant in both cases, but only in the event of hospitalization has the deviance also qualified the individual for attachment to the stereotype associated with the label "mentally ill," (assuming that hospitalization is in fact considered crucial for the stereotype, short of which an individual might only be "strange," "weird," or even "nuts," but not certified as "mentally ill"). The Freudian, presumably unconcerned with stereotyping in deciding whether or not to apply the expression "mentally ill", clearly is interested in the contextual variable "delusional" which, in this illustration, constitutes the other contextual variable.

In light of such considerations there can be no denying, as Steiner has put it, that "every understanding is actively interpretative," that "it needs decoding", and even the statements some of us confusedly think of as "literal" are freighted with significances that are not obvious.[6] Put another way, extensional translation challenges us not to be too sure we know all the angles within the extension of some expression. Some bits of subject matter are bound to be missed or passed over owing to a poor estimate of their significance; worse, the extensional associations that seem the most securely grounded often, by their very intensity, focus discourse in such a way as to distract from some other relevant feature of the subject. Thus some characterizations that should be conveyed in a translation are dropped, like the crucial role of non-hospitalization in the above hypothetical case; later they will return to haunt.

There are additional problems for the extensionalist translator, that result from the emphasis on extensions. As it is later developed, the extensional approach to translating between social science models encourages the translator to utilize, as means for refining and confirming hypothesized translations, a number of depictive representations. These depictions are to help focus attention upon certain features of the domain within which the models are applied

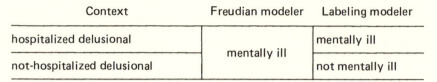

Context	Freudian modeler	Labeling modeler
hospitalized delusional	mentally ill	mentally ill
not-hospitalized delusional		not mentally ill

Figure 6

and with respect to which they are often claimed to offer incommensurable accounts. Depictions are chosen as foci for translational activities because, although they are themselves composed of symbols, these symbols are neither discursive, nor assertive, nor elements of the natural language in which the languages of the models are largely couched.

Beyond the practical difficulties involved in obtaining and manipulating suitable depictions, there is the more profound epistemological complication having to do with the way a single depiction is "read" by several viewers, for each of whom the depiction illustrates some claim or part of some claim from their own standpoint. In using depictions, a translator must be aware of the ways cultural differences effect what is seen in the depiction. However, this is precisely why depictions are the extensional technique of choice, for the translator can use these representations to determine which features of the events purportedly depicted count as within the extensions of expressions in one model but not within those of another. Presenting actual things and events instead of thing- and event-representations would not only provoke even more severe practical problems for the translator, it would mean presenting to a speaker of one model-language instances of the very state-of-affairs he either does not recognize or explicitly denies exists. Instead, the extensional translator invites the psychoanalyst or the Szaszian to entertain what are purported by the medical modelist to be depictions of a patient in an episode of mental illness caused by a biochemical imbalance, a purport ignored in the former case and denied in the latter.

Other than this we know of no formula of practical reason that the translator could "plug in" in some standard fashion. Every translator is obliged to interpret the statement at hand in the source language in the terms of the target 'anguage based upon a survey of the available information that directs and justifies a choice of interpretation. Obviously mere availability of suitable depictions is not a sufficient condition for adequate translation; the translator's understanding of the languages is necessary for this task. It too, however, may not be sufficient. Cultural differences, as noted elsewhere, are often so subtle as to elude the bilingual under ordinary conditions of discourse in either language, hence the utility of any strategy for translation.

Too great a reliance upon a strategy has its own pitfalls, though, especially in the case of the extensional translator. Too narrow a set of depictions as bases for translation may mislead either by taking the translator in a wrong direction or by causing him or her to doubt an original translational hypothesis that would have shown merit with further investigation. This seems to be a severe difficulty with extensional translation: One must have a sense when one has collected and tested the number and variety of depictions that help establish what connotations of the relevant expressions in the source and host languages do and do not hold extensionally for both. At any juncture in the translational process when this is in doubt, the translator can consult the available results of an essentialist strategy, seeking to illuminate connotations that have previously been missed and to follow them up extensionally.

Problems for Essentialist Translation

Probably the largest problem that any essentialism must face can be put in everyday terms: What is an essence for one person is excess baggage for another. In the determination of the essential concepts of a model, selection of the original account of the model is of particular importance. The account will provide the ineliminable units implicitly in the way the model is presented, but different accounts that allege to be of the same model will sometimes present different essential features. Just as the natural language translator tries to rely upon authoritative speakers of the source language, i.e., individuals whose speech habits are typical of the community and not particularly idiosyncratic, so the translator of models relies on representative speakers of the model language. However, this does not mean that the translator systematically ignores dialects. On certain occasions modes of discourse differing from the standard speech have interest in their own right. In any case, these problems touch upon both the determination of the boundaries of a model (not entirely unlike determining which languages are to be regarded as members of which language family, or which dialects relate to which language), and the selection of informants, issues facing translators generally.

The essentialist translator faces, however, a more basic problem resulting from varied readings of essences. The conclusion of Richard Cartwright's[7] essay in *The Journal of Philosophy* is worth quoting in full on this point:

> I see no reason, then, for thinking essentialism unintelligible. At the same time, I do not mean to suggest that it is without its perplexities. Chief among these is the obscurity of the grounds on which ratings of attributes as essential or accidental are to be made. Apparently, in any particular case, one is simply to reflect on the question whether the object in question could or could not have lacked the attributes in question. Now, such reflection perhaps assures us that every object is necessarily self-identical and that 9 is necessarily greater than 7. But the criteria to which one appeals in such reflection are sufficiently obscure to leave me, at least, with an embarrassingly large number of undecided cases. Is Dancer's Image necessarily or contingently a male? Necessarily or contingently a thoroughbred? And, for that matter, necessarily or contingently not a philosopher? The existence of such cases, even in such large number, does not show that there simply is no distinction between essential and accidental attributes of an object. But it does

show that the distinction is a good deal less clear than essentialists are wont to suppose.

Persons disagree about essences, it would seem, because when they reflect on questions they do so in different ways, with different abilities, or with different foci, and hence, they come to varied conclusions. If our essentialist translation strategy is to avoid this problem, we will do well to propose some common routes to inquiry, so that we minimize at least the first of these three differences. Perhaps over time the variations in abilities of translators would also be reduced, but this is not something that can be mandated in advance. Neither can we dictate which aspects of models should be the dominant foci for various investigators, though by careful specification of the claim sentence we can encourage a common domain for discourse.

The central problem, however, is this matter of the absence of techniques for essentialist inquiry. Rather than continue the tradition of simply encouraging "deep reflection" to derive essences, we will propose some preliminary tools for essentialist inquiry. Quite apart from the success or completeness of this methodology, even to propose that there are specific research techniques is to take essentialism one step away from a naive intuitionism. Once essentialists are called upon to make common moves and to present observable evidence for their claims, essentialism becomes avowedly fallibilistic. There are then grounds and occasions for appraising disparate findings among essentialist researchers who are considering purportedly the same issues or objects.

There may be multiple adequate essentialist translations, just as there are multiple adequate translations that result from other strategies, and the relative quality of translations can be evaluated. To hold otherwise—to posit that there are not essences because people disagree about essences—is to fall into a common, but unnecessary error of relativism found in a variety of related discussions. The literary analyst errs, for instance, if he suggests that there are no correct readings of a text, or that we cannot know which are correct. At the very least, if we apply his argument to his own text, we are compelled to question his conclusion. More importantly, we can point out that some readings prove more fruitful than others, include fewer contradictions per page, fit better with other (independent) readings, present more evidence, and so forth. To say as much is not to claim that there is a single, finally correct reading; as fallibilists, we would want to say the opposite, that a reading can never be known to be complete and can never absolutely be proven correct, since the reader or technology that can show it incomplete or wrong may not yet be available. The point is rather that there are grounds for judging some readings, or some claims about essences, as better than others, once the readings or essentialist analyses are conducted in comparable ways and with public evidence. Similarly, we do not care to argue that there "really are" essences, only that our techniques, which proceed as if essences exist, provide a viable route to translation.

There are more subtle problems that essentialist translators must consider, however, that result from their emphasis on relatively few elements of an object. An essentialist who studies triangles might ascertain that three sides are essential, and by trying to build understandings of triangles from this essence might come to see that the sides form angles summing to 180°, and related findings. Yet, at the same time, the person is likely to overemphasize these derivations from the essences, making triangles nothing but the extended properties of the sides, or missing other facts about triangles (e.g., those relating to planes). An essentialist translator may, similarly, overemphasize key properties of the models. For instance, certain words are likely to be used more often than others, and through the techniques to be described in Chapter 5 some of these will ordinarily be identified as essential to a model. While they may well be essential, they are likely also to carry less information than other words in the model, since it is words with wide areas of meaning that are most often repeated.[8]

We may avert some dangers that result from overemphasis by including in our translation protocol certain safeguards, such as ways to use key concepts as generative of, or building blocks in, the construction of specific claim sentences. Thus, if we were to find that "monoamine oxidase" (MAO) is essential to a biochemical model, and we were translating a claim about depression, we would want to map out how MAO is used to make the claim, rather than trying to translate MAO in its general meaning. We might find that certain types of MAO inhibitors are discussed, or that we are talking about specific MAO levels. In so doing we take not the wide application of meaning of the core concept, but rather its usage and significance in the particular case. This move also helps to preempt difficulties that arise from essential words that exhibit polysemy, or that vary in meaning with specific context.[9] In some sociological models, for example, the concept *anomie* has two meanings, one referring to a kind of normlessness in society, and the other to individuals' feelings of loss of direction. Some authors use "anomia" for the latter, in order to distinguish, but in others' works only context distinguishes. There is a further class of cases in which what is not said or what is deeply embedded in the cluster of concepts of a model is crucial to its understanding, but the careful reader will find these out.

Emphasis on essences may also result in unusual collocations. Catford[10] has proposed a distinction between cultural (or "world") differences, and collocational problems. He notes the difficulty in translating the Japanese expression, *hoteru-no yukata*, the two lexical items of which literally translate *hotel bathrobe*, a strange collocation in English. It may appear that the difference is cultural, and no doubt this is correct in the sense that a *hoteru-no yukata* is not worn by English speakers. But the difficulty in the translation presumably does not result so much from the cultural difference as from the collocation that a literal translation produces. If we explain the referent of the Japanese item using phrases that collocate pleasingly in English the difficulty diminishes.

Catford also suggests a distinction between necessarily and unnecessarily strange collocations, and the Japanese example is one where a less unusual English collocation might be employed. In some texts, however, strange collocations in the host are marks of good translations, because a similar strangeness of collocations exists in the source. Catford notes a sentence by Colette—"Le soleil allume un crépitement d'oiseaux les jardins"—in English: "The sun kindles a crackling of birds in the gardens." We might propose as parallel candidates many expressions from social science models, such as these phrases by ethnomethodologist Harold Garfinkel: "Members' accounts of everyday activities are used as prescriptions," "measures to bring particular, located features of these settings to recognizable accounts," "the coder assumes the position of a socially competent member of the arrangement that he seeks to assemble an account of," and "persons are members to organized affairs."[11] These cases seem to include both sources for unusual collocations. The model's technical terms would either obviate word-for-word (and literal) translation, or would result in difficult collocations, in a host model. At the same time, Garfinkel's collocations are far from conventional English, since we do not usually talk of assembling accounts or of being members to organized affairs, any more than we do of cracklings of birds.

Now the problem with unusual collocations is one that any type of translation must suffer; we raise the issue here because the uncareful essentialist may exacerbate the problem. By building translations from essences he is likely to produce his own unnecessarily strange collocations, by connecting words or ideas in unusual ways. The translator must keep in mind that the modelers are not themselves essentialists[12] or practicing bilingualists, and there is more to their projects than claim making. If he is to translate, he must appreciate that they talk the way they do as a result of the essences with which they work, *and* as a result of their inessential and model-idiosyncratic linguistic habits. In the above example, he would need ask whether Garfinkel is talking this way as the result of something essential to the objects of his talk or to his model, or if this talk is more indirectly related to what he is saying (e.g., he simply does not write well, or this way of talking is the fashion among ethnomethodologists).

The more general point regarding problems that result from emphasis on essences is that the essentialist translator must treat foundational features of models or objects as raw materials with which translations are built, not as grounds for reductionism, oversimplification, or unusual wording. Essences and referents are tools for the two types of translators, not the only important elements of models.

Criteria of Adequacy

Finally, before proposing our two translation strategies, let us indicate some ways in which translations between models may be judged with the same criteria as translations of natural language. Principal among these seem to be

(1) naturalness of expression, (2) retention of the force of the original, and (3) a balance of costs and benefits to the source and host.

One wants, first, for expressions in the host model to sound natural and to read without great difficulty. "The test of a real translation," J.B. Phillips has proposed, "is that it should not read like translation at all."[13] The host modeler should feel as if he is reading a claim within his own model, not something foreign to him. This does not mean that he should learn nothing from the translated claim, nor that he should feel that his own model would actually have produced such a claim. Rather, we are adapting Reuben Brower's criterion, that a good translation of a poem gives the readers what they expect in poetry. Readers of translated poetry seek the kinds of experiences that obtain in reading poems in their own language, such as certain rhythms, or the "elegancies" of an appropriate metaphor.[14] Readers of translated models seek, similarly, what their own model offers, such as insightful ways of talking and explaining, productive hypotheses, and new ways of looking at data. To bring the host modeler this feeling is not easy, however, because the source claim being translated grows out of an unique and complex web of concepts, ontology, and history of the source model. Indeed, a Kuhnian might argue that to understand another model is to operate within it, to make its unnaturalness become newly natural to oneself. But we view the models as *necessarily* unnatural to one another only in part, and we seek to minimize any *un*necessary discomfort between models.

Our two translation strategies encourage the natural expressions in the host model in several ways. We avoid in both strategies the imposition of source terms onto host models, as in a kind of transliteration. In essentialist translation, the source's claim is interpreted primarily by way of the foundational properties of the source model, and then the transfer is made on the basis of parallel developments within the host. All words used in the translated sentence come from the host. In extensionalist translation, transfer is made on the basis of host modelers' responses to queries about depictions involved in the source claim, and the queries and resulting translations are in the host's language.

More basically, we avoid foreign-sounding translations by extending our principle of charity. We assume that the source modelers talk in a way that reveals what is taken to be true within their own model, and thus, we wish to capture that sense of truth in our translations. Arthur Waley notes that translations of plays often result in queer sounding English, as in a passage that came out, "Bearing medicine given by the doctor, I, Kocho, have come. Pray tell him so." Waley points out that one might better say, "Please tell his Honor that Butterfly has come with some medicine for him from the Chief Physician." This latter version sounds natural in English and yet is faithful to the formality in the original text.

One does not have to be a literary genius in order to avoid translator's pidgin.... .
One simply has to develop the habit of hearing voices talk. The reader who cannot

consult the original will of course tend to think that "queer" English is the result of a praise-worthy fidelity to the author's idiom and may have a comforting sense that he is getting right inside the author's mind. I have even been told that translations which read well cannot possibly give a true idea of the original. But as a matter of fact when, as in the case quoted above, one compares bits of queer translation with the text, one generally finds that the oddity is completely arbitrary and represents no native idiom at all.[15]

In the case of social science models, we may not be quite correct in saying that there is little or no oddity in the original text, but we can hope even more strongly than with literary texts that none is intended. In literature an author may compose an apparently contorted passage for aesthetic reasons or because he is developing multiple levels of meaning. Sometimes religious writings have that strangeness which is mystical or oracular and should be retained. In models there are also aesthetic consideration, but the aim is above all toward true and intelligible explanations.

This first criterion of adequacy can be judged in actual translations with the measure that Martin Joos proposed: A translation is efficient to the degree that it affords maximal reception for minimal effort by the host reader.[16] The trick, however, is to accomplish such efficiency while also meeting the second criterion, retention of the force of the original source claim. Steiner has compared the relation between the translator and the source author with that of the portrait artist and her subject. In both cases the goal is to produce a new object that reveals the nature of the original subject without hindering the subject's own way of being.[17]

The power of some models appears clearly only when the model is taken as a whole. To say that suicidal persons have had difficult lives full of stressful events is at once to utter a central hypothesis of the life events model, and yet to elicit from many listeners a response of the order "No kidding!" The problem is not with the life events model (or so we would claim in following our principle of charity), but rather with taking a small piece of that model out of context. The full model purports to show a quite remarkable set of affairs, namely, that some psychiatric and somatic problems result primarily or solely from stressful life events, such as the death of one's spouse or one's children leaving home.[18] Some works within the model show in great detail not only that this postulate holds, but also the social, psychological, and physiological processes by which stress results in illness. Hence, the translator's dilemma: How to translate specific claim sentences without damaging the model in such a way that its quality and force seem to host readers less than they could.

As we shall see in the following chapters, the translator escapes this problem through various positive steps. In the example above, one might include in the claim sentence a farther reach; e.g., "Suicidal persons, to an even more extreme degree than depressives, have suffered many life events... ." And the translator would try to include some noteworthy specificity; e.g., "... Life events of the following sorts: loss of loved ones, unemployment, and frequent residential relocation." During translation efforts (once the claim sentence is developed), the translator would want to see how these claims are related to others within the model, and to the modelers' way of talking generally. Furthermore, as is exemplified in our own discussion, the translator can comment on the text or provide a gloss of the model in his own voice. In short, there are routes to success in meeting this second criterion of adequacy, but only if we recognize that it is no less important in translations of models than in any other sort of translation. To paraphrase Dante Gabriel Rossetti's decree for translators of poetry:. No good model should ever be turned into a bad one.[19]

Unfortunately, however, the third criterion interferes with fulfillment of both these first two. The first criterion (naturalness) emphasizes the host model, the second (retention of force) the source, and the third (balance) requires that we emphasize neither. By balance, we mean that costs and benefits of the source and host models should be weighed and, ideally, made equal.

The exchange of words in translations has been discussed as a commodity or financial transaction.[20] Such transactions can be justified in a variety of ways. Most simply, a transaction seems just when both parties profit; but this is impossible, at least in the long run, since after a sufficient number of rounds each party would have precisely that with which the other began. Besides two parties will not value most any item equally, because the value of an item results from its local worth and meaning as well as its broader use or exchange value. In addition, the work or inconvenience involved in the transaction must be included in any measure of exchange. In translation, the immediate labor and trouble is requested of the host modelers, who must deal with the translated sentence; the translator does the work with the source. On the other hand, depending upon the usage of the translation by the host, the source may be taxed as well, as when the host's research on the claim suggests needed revisions in the source model. The difficulty with this sort of cost is that the translator cannot know at the time whether the long run result will be improvement in the source model through these suggested revisions.

Simple equality need not be sought, however, in all transactions. Frequently we justify unequal exchanges on other ground: e.g., that one party has greater need, greater power, more to offer, or will benefit from the "interest" built up through the investment. We might want to say when translating, that a particular host is in special need of enrichment, that a model can afford to sacrifice some of its power, or conversely, that because a model is so powerful it will come out ahead regardless of the translator's efforts. In any event it is not always clear that a model loses in a transaction by giving up more than another. As Walter Benjamin has pointed out, translating too much from a text may be the greatest disservice of translators. By trying to transmit the several bits of information in a message, the translator brings to the host much that is superfluous or even misleading in the source text.[21]

Of the third criterion we might say, then, that adequacy is reached when an appropriate justification is demonstrated, to the effect that neither model is made to pay an unnecessary cost, and that potential long range benefits to the modeling of mental illness are maximized.

There are other criteria of adequacy as well, which in their sense are general, irrefutable, and well-taken as exhortations for any adequate translation, including bringing the meanings from source to host and faithfulness to the texts. But these are part and parcel of any successful execution of the task.

Notes

1. Eugene Nida, "A Framework for the Analysis and Evaluation of Theories of Translation," in Richard W. Brislin, Ed., *Translation: Applications and Research* (New York: Garden Press, 1976), p. 63.

2. *Ibid.*, p. 78.

3. Steiner, *After Babel*, p. 244.

4. Ibid., p. 244.

5. Catford, *Linguistic Theory*, p. 41.

6. Steiner, *After Babel*, p. 280.

7. Richard Cartwright, "Some Remarks on Essentialism," *The Journal of Philosophy* 65, (1968), p. 626.

8. Eugene Nida, "Principles of Translation as Exemplified by Bible Translating," pp. 27–28; and Nida, *Toward a Science*, pp. 125–127.

9. Catford, *Linguistic Theory*, pp. 95–96.

10. *Ibid.*, p. 101–103.

11. Hardol Garfinkel, *Studies in Ethnomethodology*, pp. 1–34.

12. Their theories may be essentialist, however, as in the case of the Freudian theory. See Charles Rycroft, *A Critical Dictionary of Psychoanalysis* (New York: Basic Books, 1968), p. 46. Similar observations hold for the extensional translator.

13. As quoted in Nida, *Toward a Science*, p. 163.

14. Reuben Brower, "Seven Agamemnons," in Reuben Brower, ed., *On Translation*, p. 174.

15. Arthur Waley, "Notes on Translation," *Delos* 2, (1969), p. 163.

16. As quoted in Nida, *Toward a Science*, p. 182.

17. Steiner, *After Babel*, p. 267.

18. See footnote 3 of Chapter 6.

19. As quoted in Poggioli, "The Added Artificer," p. 143.

20. E.g., Marc Shell, "Money and the Mind," *Modern Language Notes* 95, (1980): 516–562; and Claude Levi-Strauss, *Structural Anthropology* (New York: Basic Books, 1963).

21. Benjamin, *Illuminations*.

4

Extensional Translation

In this chapter we develop what we shall call an "extensional" translation strategy. After some remarks on extensionalism in the theory of reference and the philosophy of language we discuss an extensional semantic theory in order to gain some clues for designing a translation strategy. Finally the program of an extensional translation between models is explored. In general, it will help to recall through the preliminary discussion that we look forward to developing a strategy for translation that does not entail commitment to the ontology of any particular model, but attempts to isolate common references for expressions in each model by means of exposing informants to certain conditions of stimulation.

Presumably one important obstacle to discourse among proponents of the various psychiatric models is the lack of agreement as to what sorts of entities there are to be talked about relative to etiology, pathology, and epidemiology. Although some may dismiss the obstacle as "political," that charge cannot be evaluated unless there are techniques for ameliorating disputes about basic reference. To what extent, for example, do behavioral and psychoanalytic evaluations of a particular case resist comparison and communion due to uncertainties about the degree to which the two accounts are talking about the same thing, rather than mere dogmatism by proponents of each? If the incommensurability thesis (IT) discussed in Chapter 1 has any force at all, there is good cause for concern about the influence of scientifically irrelevant considerations upon selection of a mental illness model. For in the absence of means for identifying agreed upon features of the domain that is the object of discourse, model selection is possibly arbitrary and probably devisive. One of the salient features of the extensional translation strategy is the withholding of commitment to a particular ontology while taking advantage of the dispositions of informants representing the several models to agree to some minimal standards for cross-identification of referents alluded to by the technical language of each model.

It will be recalled that according to a Kuhnian version of IT, there is doubt about the status of a common world for different paradigms or models to refer to, though in his 1970 Postscript Kuhn holds out the possibility of translation. In a Quinean version of IT, on the other hand, a common world is explicitly retained, at least insofar as there is some source of sensory stimulation, but incommensurability seems invited by a concept of meaning as something to be shared. Yet, we have suggested, since some notion of a common world is left us, there may be a basis for translation even though usual uses of meanings are not relied upon. The extensionalist translation strategy takes advantage of this possibility; on the other hand, the strategy will have to be guided in its design by a problem called the "inscrutability of reference," to be discussed later on. Hence our concrete techniques for extensional translation will be devised in light of the apparent limitations of our usual notions of meaning, both the intuitive variety and that which relies on simple pointing for ascertaining meaning.

The most obvious target of Quine's attack on usual ideas about meaning is an uncritical semantic theory which relies on what he characterizes as the myth of the museum.[1] On this view words are labels pegged to meanings that are themselves exhibits in a sort of mental museum, each meaning a particular mental entity. But IT purports to show that a sentence in a model-language knows no particular meaning assignment, since the model's sentences can be interpreted in various ways so long as the whole fits the available evidence. If this is correct, then there seem to be no meanings in *this* sense to use as ways of comparing the meaning-parts of one model with allegedly analogous meaning-parts of another model. But then, IT went, how can models be measured against one another at all?

We do not wish to engage in a discussion concerning the validity of the indeterminacy thesis, since it was introduced only to establish a degree of intelligibility and plausibility for the claim that there is incommensurability among modes of discourse in scientific models. In a related vein, an extensional semantics will be seen to avoid appeal to synonymy relations in a language and will substitute a notion of likeness of meaning. But no argument against the synonymy of terms within a natural language or among several is addressed *per se*. As we have suggested earlier, there is a sense in which it is worthwhile to see if one can get along, as semanticist or translator, without positing synonymy relations. This may not in fact be possible for pure semantics ultimately, or even for actual translation entirely, but we want to pursue this avenue so far as it allows for purposes of translation.

Hence our interest in extensional semantics is strictly limited to those *guidelines* it can provide for an extensional translation strategy. The present legitimacy or future prospects of any semantic theory, including extensional semantics, is irrelevant to us save as those considerations bear upon practical refinements in extensional translation. Another way of putting this is to say that our guidelines for translations but *not* our theoretical criteria of meaning-fulness are found in extensional semantics. For the latter we are willing to entertain any received theory of meaning.

In the present section we set out some fundamental considerations of an extensional translation strategy from the standpoint of the philosophy of language. In the next section the nature of the semantic theory itself and some of its technical apparatus is described, although no finished theory is presented. While the theory awaits full systematization, its outlines are clear enough for suggestion of some translation guidelines.[2] Even were no extensional semantic theory completable, the extensional translator *qua* translator could legitimately utilize a strategy inspired by an incipient extensional semantic. In fact, the extensional translator can do his or her job so long as the guidelines for application of extensional translation principles in the field, and the principles themselves, are consistent with whatever semantic theory he or she holds.[3] As we shall see, the weak relation of extensionality and meaning mentioned above does not represent any particular psychological account of meaning, but an epistemological thesis of the kind of a rational reconstruction.

Extensionalism: Some Preliminaries

Our discussion of extensional semantics can begin by treating the question of criteria of sameness of meaning. The suggestion is that two terms have the same meaning if and only if they apply to exactly the same things. This is not a definition of meaning, for that would identify extensionality with meaning. Rather, this is a weaker claim concerning the conditions which obtain such that, if two predicates have the same extension, then they have the same meaning, and the reverse.

One should not confuse the extensionality condition for sameness of meaning of two terms with Alfred Tarski's truth definition or its descendents. Briefly stated, Tarski held that a definition could be given for a language if there were a rule schema such that for each sentence S of the language and p for truth conditions of that sentence this formula can accurately be predicted:

$$S \text{ is true if and only if } p.$$

Although Tarski was talking about formal languages, Davidson[4] has proposed that this formula for a theory of truth can be applied as the basis for a theory of meaning for natural languages. Tarski's truth formula as applied to an English sentence, "Snow is white," holds of course that "Snow is white" is true if and only if snow is white where "Snow is white" is S and that snow is white is p are the conditions that would guarantee the truth of S. Now Davidson's suggestion amounts to the meaning formula or equation

$$S \text{ means that } p = S \text{ is true if and only if } p.$$

Without entering in a lengthy discussion of this proposal we can fruitfully note one serious objection, namely that while p may guarantee the *truth* of S, p need not satisfy us that it also provides an account of the *meaning* of S. Kempson[5] has pointed out that "Snow is white" is true if and only if grass is green is allowed by the truth formula, but the string "grass is green" can hardly be said to "guarantee the meaning" of "Snow is white" even though the substitution for S and p in the truth formula is allowable. Rather, the meaning equation must be rewritten so as to restrict the set of conditions guaranteeing the truth of a sentence to those conditions that are both necessary and sufficient for the truth of that sentence. The more restrictive formula reads

S means that p = necessarily S is true if and only if p.

Unfortunately this revision invites the morass of problems Quine[6] has adduced regarding the concept of necessity in the semantics of natural language, namely analytic truth.[7] Generally, the difficulty is that necessary truth is analyzed in terms of logical truth, which is itself analyzed in terms of the laws of logic, which are explained by a notion of logical truth, hence a vicious circularity.

This digression is meant to distinguish the extensionality condition from the revised and restricted version of Tarski's formula à la Davidson, for the former does not propose to be yet another version of a truth-based theory of meaning. First, the extensionality condition describes not one sentence but two terms (or, later, sentences) A and B such that

A and B have the same meaning if and only if they have the same extension.

Second, there is no mention of truth in the extensionality formula. Sameness of meaning is a matter of the applicability of A and B to the same things, not of the truth of both or either. A and B need not truly assert anything in order to be applicable. That A *applies* to x is indeed true or false, but that A is *true of* x does not follow from the fact that A applies to x. The one-word sentence "Unicorn" may apply to a representation of a unicorn but not be true of the representation. In fact it is literally false since no representation of a unicorn is a unicorn. Since we want to avoid prejudicial commitment to the existence of some sorts of entities asserted by some models and not others, this is not a trivial consideration. Therefore, third, there is no problem of analyticity in this formula since A and B can apply to exactly the same things without that co-extensionality being true necessarily for A and B. All descriptions of bachelors may also be taken as descriptions of unmarried men[8] without commitment to the often alleged analyticity of "A bachelor is an unmarried man."

This is not to suggest that there are no problems in the extensionality formula to be worked out. In particular, to say that A and B have the same extension is to say that A and B are *about* exactly the same things, and it is not always easy to tell what a sentence is about.[9] But this is a different sort of problem from that of analytic truth. Hence it is erroneous to identify a truth-based semantics with our extensionality condition for sameness of meaning.[10]

On the other hand, our extensionality condition does require specification of a set of conditions for the certification of sameness of meaning, so to that minimal degree it bears a resemblance to a semantics of truth conditions. But it is immune to the major apparent disadvantage of the latter as against speech act semantics, which is that a semantics of truth conditions seems limited to treating declarative utterances and not interrogative or imperative utterances.[11] As our project concerns expressions from two or more modes of scientific discourse, we can well be satisfied to let imperatives and interrogatives go and limit ourselves to certain declaratives, especially those we have called claim sentences. Of course, we will have to have an apparatus that renders our extensionality condition for two terms applicable to treatment of pairs of strings of terms and pairs of sentences. We can begin to reckon with this and other strategic translation problems by surveying the prospects for extensional semantics.

The Nature of an Extensional Semantic Theory

If the two nouns apply to exactly the same things, they are said to have the same *primary extension*. Consider the terms "triangular figure" and "trilateral figure." Clearly they have the same extension, since any triangular figure will be a trilateral figure and vice versa, so the terms do apply to exactly the same things. However, it is apparent that the terms do not have the same meaning, so an extensional semantics, if it is to be at all adequate with respect to ordinary usage, must "capture" this difference in meaning. Alternatively we can note that the terms "unicorn" and "centaur" are ordinarily counted by logicians as having the same extension, namely null, yet clearly they differ in meaning. A Szaszian modelist manages to talk meaningfully albeit disparagingly about expressions like "paranoid schizophrenic" and "delusionary psychotic" even though in her view those terms fail to refer. In this view there is really nothing at all in the primary extension of these terms, although the "mental illness establishment" thinks there is. In this case that the two terms differ in meaning must be accounted for on some ground other than their primary extensions, since they share the same null primary extension, unless we are to impose an inappropriate ontology on the Szaszian.

In an extensionalist approach the difference in meaning in these cases can be accounted for by noting that representations (descriptions and depictions) of unicorns are not representations of centaurs. In order to avoid the impression there is existential quantification over "unicorns" and "centaurs," we construct one-place predicates (i.e., predicates that do not take objects) as stipulative correctives to the illusion suggested by the apparently two-place predicate "represents." Thus, unicorn-representations and centaur-representations constitute the *secondary extension* of "unicorn" and "centaur," respectively. Now we have an extensionalist criterion of synonymy: Two terms are synonymous just in case their primary and secondary extensions are the same.[12] Since the secondary extensions of "unicorn" and "centaur" differ, the terms are not synonymous. This accounts for the nonsynonymy of terms with null or doubtful primary extension from an extensionalist standpoint.

However, synonymy turns out to be too strong under extensional semantics, and needs to be replaced by a notion of likeness of meaning. For under the extensional synonymy criterion any two different words (the replicas of two different words) must differ in meaning. This is not disconcerting in cases like "triangular figure" and "trilateral figure," for they do seem to differ in meaning although they share primary extension. That they differ in meaning although alike in primary extension is covered by the fact that the secondary extension of "triangular figure" includes "a triangular figure which is not a trilateral figure," which is a triangular figure-representation but not a trilateral figure-representation. But if we consider the generalization of this conclusion, any two word-events that are not replicas of each other must differ in meaning. For example, "even prime" and "two" could not be synonymous in a strict extensional semantic account since, "Even prime that is not a two," is an even prime-representation but not a two-representation.

This is a result in extensional semantics. We can limit the effect of this result, if we wish, by regarding descriptive representations of the form

P that is not a Q

uninteresting on the grounds that for a certain P and a certain Q only a contrived example of this form is capable of distinguishing between the senses of P and Q. An analogous treatment can be afforded all depictive representations of P and Q similarly contrived to try to show their nonsynonymy. In this fashion extensional semanticists can perhaps save synonymy if they wish. Rolf Eberle[13] in his development of Goodman's theory of reference into an extensional semantics does not commit himself to the antisynonymy doctrine, which has been attacked by Jerold Katz[14] among others.

As extensional translators, however, there is no reason to enter the fray, for we have already given up attempts to determine whether two terms share in primary extension, which is half of the extensional requirement for synonymy cited above. Whether or not two terms have the same primary extension is precisely the question that extensional translation sets aside, for it is agnostic as to whether there are in fact any such things for the terms in question to apply to. Our interest is in determining the degree of agreement concerning the secondary extension of claim sentences, the degree to which two purported objects can be represented by the same depictions. We will see that no descriptions can be in the common secondary extension of claim sentences from different models because all descriptions for each claim sentence will be in the language of its model, and our informants *qua* informants will only know their own language. Using depictive representations as aids and justification devices, the extensional translator's job is to help informants from two different modes of discourse to know when and to what degree they are talking about the same purported objects, not to certify the existence of those multiply represented objects. Thus we strive to specify degrees of likeness of meaning of expressions from two different model-languages, via those representative objects that fall in their secondary extension. For example, a claim sentence from a psychoanalytic model is to be analyzed for those objects in its secondary extension. It will be alike in meaning with a claim sentence from, say, a social model to the extent that the latter claim sentence can be analyzed in terms of the *same depictions* in *its* secondary extension.

The recognition of secondary extensions came about by way of distinguishing between the meanings of two terms with null primary extension, "unicorn" and "centaur", and in order to distinguish between two terms with identical primary extensions that nonetheless differ in meaning, "triangular figure" and "trilateral figure". The upshot permits us to avoid imposing unfriendly ontological commitments on Szaszians, for instance, whose talk of "paranoid schizophrenia" is admitted as of some thing that logically could exist but, on their view, happens in fact not to exist. But such things can be analyzed in terms of secondary extensions. Thus for any noun x its secondary extension includes all x-representations. These x-representations are themselves obvious portions of the world of native speaker and translator, while the primary extension of x may not be an obvious portion of the world for the informant who does not believe in unicorns or paranoid schizophrenia, or who does not know the meaning of the term for an informant from another language community. The extensional translator therefore has in principle a device for relating some term to another by way of associating representative objects that are in both of their secondary extensions, without reference to abstract entities such as thoughts, ideas, or intensions of any sort, and without prejudice to the question whether some term actually refers, i.e., has anything in its primary extension.[15]

An Extensional Translation Strategy

The formal purpose of extensional translation is to determine whether some depictive representations are in both secondary extensions of expressions from alternate modes of discourse. This strategy avoids commitment to the ontology of either language, since our criteria of translatability have to do with thing-representations rather than with the things themselves. This recalls one of the original motivations for an account of meaning according to secondary extensions: the specification of objects in the extension of expressions, originally count nouns and predicates, with null denotation. This strategy is in like manner applicable for any expressions the denotation of which is a matter of doubt.

Our own translation program could be expected to address claim sentences from the medical model such as, "John is a hypochondriac; he is preoccupied with suspicions of serious disease due to a certain chemical imbalance associated with obsessive behavior." From the standpoint of at least some nonmedical models it is doubtful that there is any state of affairs purportedly described by this claim sentence. Without commitment to the existence of this state of affairs *as described*, we may try to compile a set of depictions of this purported state of affairs or of significant components of this purported state of affairs. The depictions could be videotaped interviews, films illustrative of the purported condition, or such. Those representations that are not ontologically prejudicial, constitute aids for determining the degree to which the claim sentence is translatable into one from another model; or we may have to work piecemeal in a phrase-by-phrase fashion. Our hope for some degree of translatability in general rests on a notion of overlap; for example, that a medical modelist and a social modelist can agree that what counts for the former as "obsessive behavior" is operative in the state of affairs even though the latter does not recognize "obsessive behavior" as having anything in its primary extension.

Of course there are practical considerations that endorse this approach. Actual cases can hardly be trotted out at the will of the translator and exhibited as applicability conditions to informants for testing hypothesized translations. Depictions also help in narrowing down those features of the purported subject or state of affairs that are taken by an informant to justify application of a particular term or sentence. Further, while it is not easy to tell what the primary extension of some general terms like "hypochondriasis" is supposed to be, the complex of conditions they refer to should be representable. The isolation of these conditions for representation is admittedly a challenge to the ingenuity of the translator and the patience of the informant, as we have already noted.

Eberle[16] has explicated two primitive relations for two or more representative objects; that is, objects that represent the same purported subject. In the language of secondary extension we shall call these x-representations or more precisely x-descriptions where x is a place-holder for some purported subject. We will specify these primitive relations and then modify them for our own needs, keeping in mind that our claim sentences, unlike those of interest to Eberle, *may* in fact denote even though our task as translators is not to determine whether they do or do not.

Consider the denotationless nouns "Venus" and "Aphrodite." A semantics of secondary extension characterizes this pair as an instantiation of the primitive relation of having the same (purported) subject, a relation Eberle calls *homotopical*. Thus all Venus-representations and all Aphrodite-representations are homotopical, as they have the same (purported) subject.

A semantics of secondary extension not only assumes a relation between two x-depictions having the same thing-like subject, but also between two x-depictions having the same state-of-affairs-like subject, a relation Eberle calls *homothematical*.

Our extensional translation strategy also includes two kinds of primitive relation, with differences shaped by the following considerations. First, we are interested in specifying the degree to which expressions from different modes of discourse have the same thing-like or state-of-affairs-like subject, if at all, since homotopicality or homothematicality requires agreement that the expressions do or do not in fact denote (i.e., have any objects in their primary extension); whereas our concern as extensional translators is the determination of a minimum degree to which the expressions share the same subject when that is constituted by a set of objects in the secondary extension of both expressions. Therefore, secondly, our process of likeness-of-subject measurement requires the introduction of a set of representations for both of the expressions in question. This set of representations in turn provides the reference point for gaining experimental specification of degrees of likeness-of-subject. Hence the primitive relations guiding the extensional translation strategy can be expressed:

paratopic—the primitive relation of having the same thing-like subject to an (experimentally) specific degree.

parathematic—the primitive relation of having the same state-of-affairs-like subject to an (experimentally) specificable degree.

Let A and B be expressions, say count nouns for the sake of simplicity, from two different modes of discourse. Their secondary extensions include A-depictions and B-depictions. A and B are paratopical only to the experimentally specifiable degree that A-depictions turn out, upon trials with suitable informants, also to be B-depictions, and vice versa. Each trial consists in placing before the informant qualified in that mode of discourse a certain stimulus condition, say an A-depiction, accompanied by a suitable query such as "A?" Assent will be recorded as evidence for applicability of A to that representational object. Those representations that turn out to be judged by the translator to be assertable as both A-depictions and B-depictions constitute the coreferentiality or *overlap* of the secondary extensions of A and B, the minimum degree to which they share the same thing-like subject.

The following diagrammatic example (see Figure 7) should give a sense of what we are striving for.

The more representational objects there are in the overlap, the greater the minimum degree of paratopicality or parathematicality. In the diagram only expressions in the object languages are those between quotation marks. All others are in the technical vocabulary of the translator (Greek mythology, Roman mythology, Aphrodite-representations, Venus-representations, overlap, goddess-of-love depictions). Areas 1 and 3 contain descriptions as well as depictions, while Area 2 contains only depictions. The reason for this is that Aphrodite-depictions could also be Venus-depictions, or at least those depictions that do not exhibit stylistic traits peculiar to the depictions of either Greek or Roman deities. But the description "goddess of love," while both an Aphrodite- and a Venus-description, has replicas in the language of both Greek and Roman mythology. However, IT debars us from assuming that

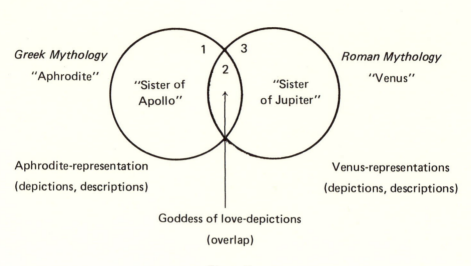

Figure 7

"goddess of love" in one system of expressions is synonymous with "goddess of love" in another system of expressions, or any homonymous expressions in different systems, because each replica of "goddess of love" is "model-laden" or infused with the meaning-relations inherent in that system.[17] No such problem exists concerning Aphrodite- or Venus-*depictions*, since these depictions do not appear in the terms of either object language.

This last observation seems to recommend the introduction of a meta-language besides the technical vocabulary of the translator to couch the descriptive representations in the secondary extensions of both expressions we seek to translate. We have some of the same problems with a meta-language that we noted in Chapter 2 regarding a meta-model. The meta-language would have to be learned by all informants from each object language in order for them to understand and respond to the descriptions. This would beg the question of translating, or at least permit us to assume our way out of the technical difficulties of translation, since the informant could as easily learn how to speak in terms of the other model without a "go-between" language. Further, the translator would then have to be not merely bilingual but trilingual, and translators ordinarily need to be only bilingual in order to translate from one language into another, except perhaps at the outer reaches of novel translation where multilinguals are needed for tracing of cognates.

Rather than assume a question-begging and artificially introduced meta-language, we had better return to the actual practice of translation for clues on how to proceed. A translator works by gathering together as many of the connotations of a particular expression from a source language as is practicable. The extensional translator conducts this gathering procedure by constructing descriptions or depictions in the source language and obtaining assent. In this fashion "sister of Apollo" and "goddess of love," also in the source language, can both be determined to be in the secondary extension of "Aphrodite," as can a number of appropriate depictions. At this phase the translator can also work between descriptions and depictions to determine a set of potential depictions for the overlap, those that seem well associated in that language with the Aphrodite-descriptions as well as with "Aphrodite."

Next, the translator searches for an expression in the host language which applies to an analogous range of representational objects. For example, "sister of Jupiter" is analogous to "sister of Apollo," for Aphrodite as sister of Apollo-descriptions will resemble Venus as sister of Jupiter-descriptions relatively more than anything else in the language, just as would man-descriptions in English be found to be similar to homme-descriptions in French.

Now the translator can test the initial hypothesis of translatability by exposing an informant from the host language to the set of well-confirmed Aphrodite-depictions. Those that yield assent to the query "Venus?" count as Venus-depictions as well as Aphrodite-depictions and so constitute the minimum degree of paratopicality for "Aphrodite" and "Venus", i.e., the overlap. Some of these depictions will perhaps be particularly associated with certain Aphrodite-descriptions, as will some of the Aphrodite-depictions that did not qualify for the overlap. By attending to those depictions that did and did not qualify for the overlap, the translator can eliminate some hypothesized similarities. In other words, some connotations will simply not hold for both expressions each in their own language. What count as depictions of one expression but not another sensitize the translator to those connotative differences, or in terms of extensional translation, to differences in the applicability conditions of the expressions.

Unfortunately, this example is mythological in more ways than one, albeit relatively straightforward. Our next step is to take a claim sentence and walk through a hypothetical translation. Much will be assumed in this example but its purpose is not to persuade of the adequacy of the "conclusion" but rather to illustrate further the mechanics of extensional translation. (In Chapters 6 and 7, we work out an actual translation.)

Consider a claim sentence from a medical model, to be translated into a social model.

> Joe is a hypochondraic; he is preoccupied with a suspicion of serious disease, and this suspicion is due to a chemical imbalance.

First, the translator gathers a number of appropriate depictions of significant units of the claim sentence: Hypochondraic-depictions of a general order including some disease preoccupation-depictions, some chemical imbalance-depictions and some obsessive behavior-depictions. Presumably all of these will yield ready assent from an informant in the medical model to the query "Hypochondraic?" but the chemical imbalance-depiction will not yield ready assent to "Disease preoccupation?" and relatively delayed assent to "Obsessive behavior?" In this fashion the translator is armed with depictions of various aspects of this part of the "world" of the medical modelist.

Next, the depictions (which as we said can include films, photographs, videotapes, slides, etc.) are presented to the social modelist. It is unlikely that the social modelist would assent to any queries in his own language with respect to chemical imbalance-depictions, with the possible exception of "Primary deviant?"[18] However, some members of the other sets of depictions would certainly yield assent to queries such as "Prinary deviant?", "Anti-normative behavior?", "Anti-normative concern with own well-being?", "Inter-nalized hypochondraic's role?", etc. The translator records which queries in each language share which set of depictive representations. These represent their partial applicability conditions, their paratopicality.

The extensional translator does not diagram claim sentences in the fashion of the essentialist, by searching for essential conditions for significant units of a source language claim sentence. Instead, the extensional translator attends to the sorts of events that the speaker of a certain model-language seems to presuppose as conditions for the application of the claim sentence, including those mentioned in relevant textual discussions. Some of these the translator will know by means of that minimal competence in the language that qualifies him as a bilingual; others the translator can gather by inspecting the model's textbook descriptions or dictionary definitions that elaborate the subject matter of the expressions in the claim sentence. Within the model these can be tested by presenting them to informants and querying so as to determine whether or not these descriptive representations are indeed within the sec-ondary extensions of the expressions the translator is concerned with. The descriptions are entered into a diagram as markers according to their generality with respect to one another. Without access to the process whereby the diagrams were divised, there may in fact be no obvious difference between those of the extensionalist and the essentialist. The major difference, besides the assumptions under which the diagrams are developed, are the claims made by each sort of translator concerning what the markers actually stand for, either essential conditions or applicability conditions of the claim sentence.

Then the translator consults the diagram for this claim sentence in the source language, the medical model (see Chapter 2). Let us say it includes the fragment shown in Figure 8. If there are paratopical expressions in the social model for the markers strongly associated in the diagram, these can then be constructed into a grammatical expression in that model. For instance, in the labeling model the translator might produce:

Joe is a primary deviant; his concern with his physical well-being is taken by others to be abnormal. Biochemists attribute the cause of his primary deviance to a chemical imbalance.

The hypothetical results may seem trivial to proponents of either or both models. The medical modelist might complain that biochemists not only

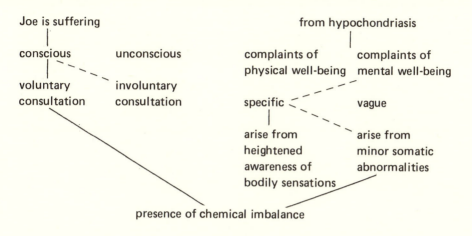

Figure 8

attribute cause to the chemical imbalance but correctly do so—that hypo-chondraisis *is* a chemical imbalance. And the labeling theorist might express disinterest in the primary deviation, claiming that many things could be labeled, and it is the *usage* of the label that is interesting.

These objections do not indicate the triviality of the extensionalist's host sentence, however. Triviality of the sentence can be determined by its use. For example, if the labeling theorist explores the claim and finds that post-labeling the hypochondriac ceases to be so concerned with his well-being, becomes more concerned, or exhibits another change in biochemistry, he might have reason to argue the triviality of the sentence (though the translation may nevertheless be the best possible). From the other direction, if the medical modelist can show that hypochondriasis is only or primarily the result of a chemical imbalance, he might have reason to argue triviality.

One possible outcome of translation is that the host finds the translated material trivial, but hopefully this is a finding based upon inquiry rather than prejudice or protection of turf. The English reader of Proust who finds upon detailed study that the novelist is in fact inappropriately obstruse is to be distinguished from the schoolboy who is protecting his own free time or masculine image with his peers by calling the work "sissy."

In fact the medical modelist *qua* medical modelist could not escape some degree of misunderstanding of the social model's claim sentence. Whatever understanding he seems to have is based upon the appearance in both his and the social model of natural language expressions, but even these are not necessarily synonymous to what seem to be the same expressions in his own model language. so in his role as advocate of a certain model, he can hardly avoid prejudicial interpretation of a language whose claims he does not understand. When a medical modelists reads the clause "biochemists attribute the cause," he is unlikely to appreciate that the labeling theorist's relativism does not permit him to say that something *is*, and that the labeling theorist treats even his own factual claims as "readings."

In quite another sense "triviality" is not the mark of a poor translation but of an excellent one. For the above case the translation of a medical model claim sentence into a social model seemed trivial to the medical modelist in the sense of unimportance. But in another sense of trivial a good translation is obvious to a speaker of the host language *in situ*, assuming an appropriate level of observationality. Similarly, an unprejudiced bilingual would find a good translation of a claim sentence into the host language trivial in the latter sense. As Quine has pointed out, "[f]or translation theory, banal messages are the breath of life."[19]

Our interest in translation is not the achievement of translation alone but also the establishment of a basis for identifying conceptions in a model that are resistent to translation. In the extensional strategy this basis is constituted by those depictions of components of the source model that do not permit a reasonably efficient application of an expression in the host model-language. By the same token, the markers that suggest nonoverlapping depictions in the diagram of the source claim sentence indicate those features of the ontology of the source model that distinguish it from that of the host model. In extensional terms these depictions represent conditions of nonparatopicality, or the limits of the mutual applicability of expressions from different model-languages.

As to the applicability conditions of expressions gleaned from query-assent trials with depictions, they are guides for the translator in formulating efficient interpretations of a claim sentence or its units in the terms of another model. This notion does not do the same job as the notion of stimulus conditions does for Quine,[20] for these are taken to explicate a speaker's dispositions to verbal behavior. These dispositions are in turn taken by Quine to *be* the language of a speaker. Whether Quine is right or not, certainly we do not hold that the applicability conditions give even a partial account of a speaker's language, but rather that our expectations concerning its issue can be refined by attending to certain relevant, albeit often contrived, conditions of stimulation. How the applicability conditions manage thus to assist in translation can be treated in various theories of translation. Moreover, as Chomsky[21] points out, the query in the query-assent strategy that both we and Quine borrow from anthropological linguistics itself counts as part of Quine's stimulus conditions for radical translation, but is hardly present in those arbitrary stimulus conditions Quine thinks more generally call forth verbal behavior. Therefore we do not wish to deny the artificiality of our experimental setting or claim that the applicability conditions for claim sentences that arise through this experimentation are more than aids in justification and clues to assist translation.

The extensional translator's strategy is a near-relation of what Quine has called the method of "semantic ascent":

Semantic ascent, as I speak of it, applies anywhere. "There are wombats in Tasmania" might be paraphrased as "'Wombat' is true of some creatures in Tasmania," if there were any point to it... The strategy of semantic ascent is that it carries the discussion into a domain where both parties are better agreed to the objects (*viz.*, words) and on the main terms concerning them. Words, or their inscriptions, unlike points, miles, classes, and the rest, are tangible objects of the size so popular in the marketplace, where men of unlike conceptual schemes communicate at their best. The strategy is one of ascending to a common part of two fundamentally disparate conceptual schemes, the better to discuss the disparate foundations.[22]

But instead of shifting from talking of objects to talking of words, the extensional translator shifts from talking of things to talking of thing-representations. This shift is related to Quine's semantic ascent in the obvious respect that both seek to carry discussions between proponents of different conceptual schemes into a more agreeable domain. However, the extensional translator's strategy is not meant to ground discussion of the "disparate foundations" of the conceptual schemes, but rather to identify relatively gross contexts of common experience that could aid in determining which expressions from two conceptual models apply in such cases. An extensionalized semantic account is not interested in whether "'Wombat' is true of some creatures in Tasmania" but rather if "Wombat" *applies* to some creatures in Tasmania. More particularly, our secondarily extensionalized semantic account directs attention to those thing-representations in the presence of which "Wombat?" yields assent from those who should know, even short of the presence of the things themselves.

We have hardly noted the severe technical problems that confront the translator in adjusting depictions in order to qualify a claim sentence, or its significant units, for translation into another model by means of co-extensionality. But these problems should not be confused with the additional disconcerting epistemological problems associated with what Quine has called the inscrutability of reference.[23] In formulating IT along Quinean lines we alluded to the origins of translational indeterminacy in a context of radical translation. Subsequently the indeterminacy thesis was adjusted to more common translational conditions that gave it at least a theoretical force and made it a practical *caveat* to those who would assume commensurability owing to a naive notion of shared meanings. Were we operating under conditions of *radical* translation, with no historic contact between the "culture" of the models at hand, then not only would indeterminacy be a more immediate issue but the task of determining when two predicates have common extensions would prove equally recalcitrant, since behavioral dispositions to refer also have indeterminate interpretations. Now, as extensional translators we are sensitive enough to the indeterminacy in our theoretical background not to interpret "same extension" as "same meaning," and in any case we dropped such pretensions when we gave up primary extensions as foci for translation. And as translators we assume bilingualism, i.e., the historic and implicit selection of a particular translation manual on grounds that can be described as pragmatic, without denying the residual force of IT but co-existing with it.

So our stand on the inscrutability of reference is that it casts a shadow over translation in the field that is complementary to that of indeterminacy. Both shadows keep us in the dark only insofar as we recall that the way we learn to work between languages, whatever our theory of language-learning happens to be, was nonetheless an implicit selection of a particular translation manual among others. Quine grants that "within the parochial limits of our own language, we can continue as always to find extensional talk clearer than intensional" for the apparatus of individuation in the language can then be regarded as fixed.[24] Surely once we have learned two languages we can be as parochial in one as in the other, can refer as well in one as in the other, for the individuative apparatus is then as fixed for us in one as in the other. Thus the extensional translator knows to what depictions he is referring from the standpoint of each model. Assent to depictions by informants from each model justifies claims of co-referenciality and establishes common applicability conditions for certain claim sentences, and this is in part owing to the fact that as translators we are bilinguals, regardless of how bilingualism is accounted for.

A further difference between a context of radical translation between models and our own situation is that according to a Quinean IT we could in principle give a complex enough interpretation of any claim sentence in one model in the language of another model so that *all* behavioral dispositions of speakers of both model-languages were satisfied, including dispositions to assent to all of the same depictive representations. However, since as translators our goal is not extensional equivalence for its own sake, we are content to leave Quine's claim untested.

In a context of nonradical translation we seek those translations that are most likely to gain assent from informants without protest of complexity than those among a countless number of unwieldy and circuitous translations Quine claims could be devised. Translators are quite willing to forego "extensional equivalence at all costs" for efficiency in other respects, especially for the satisfaction of their monolingual clients that the "gist" of a statement in another language has been conveyed, or enough to suit a limited purpose under certain conditions.

Hence, the extensional translator's problems of extension are more like the everyday confusions that inhibit communication between speakers within a language, since, again, the translator is a bilingual. In these contexts reference is managable even if not properly scrutable to a Quinean. The pointing, whether verbal or physical, that the translator does to a depiction in the presence of an informant is liable to the usual slings and arrows of misunderstanding, but expressions of puzzlement on the face or in the language of the informant are clear-cut clues that something has gone awry. Far more troublesome are those misunderstanding that get systematically embedded in the translator's construal of what the informant is willing and unwilling to assent to as a hypothetically equivalent characterization to that in another language of a certain depiction. Without guarantees of infallibility the translator has good reason to suppose, and in any case must hope, that continued investigation of a web of related expressions will tend to reveal such errors.

Working with Informants

There are three phases in work with informants. In the first, the translator is concerned to secure an understanding of the source-language by checking which x-descriptions are appropriate for the application of some expression. (Depictions may also be used to work within a language but in that case their use corresponds to that in phase two). The source expression (which could be all or part of a claim sentence) is checked for descriptions that fall in its secondary extension by presenting the expression and querying based on the x-description to gradually more specific levels. If the source expression is quite mysterious to the translator, the query procedure begins with the highest set of distinctions, i.e., "Entity?", "Event?", "Abstract?". If there is assent only to "Entity?", let us say, querying continues based on the next more specific level of x-description, i.e., "Inanimate?", "Animate?". If there is assent to "Animate?", for example, querying continues with "Animal?", "Human?", etc. This categorial hierarchy of semantic domains is familiar to translators[25] and is here adapted to increasing levels of specificity for descriptions in the secondary extension of the source expression. The process continues in this fashion until the translator is confident of results that coordinate with his or her diagram of this expression or until that diagram has been sufficiently ramified by the procedure to admit an attempt at translation.

The second phase of work with informants calls for the selection of depictions that the translator believes represent the pattern of interpretations of the source expression in phase one. These are checked with source language informants by presenting them along with suitable queries. Now these depictions are the "referencial foci" of the translation being attempted.

In the third phase host language informants are presented with the depictions and queried in the host language as the translator hypothesizes to be appropriate. If the hypothesized translations do not meet ready assent, the same procedures as outlined in phase one can be followed, this time with depictions as the objects of queries from the most general semantic domain desired downward. And of course the queries are made in the host language this time. The translator's purpose is to obtain a refined set of descriptions in the host language based on the host language informant's reactions to the depictions, and then fit this set of descriptions into a host language characterization of the depictions. Then the diagram of the source expression is consulted so as to determine the arrangement of host descriptions in a proposed translation of the claim sentence.

In all three phases the translator seeks assent or dissent to his queries. More precisely, what elicits one of these responses is the combination of a prompting stimulation (the source expression in phase one, depictions in phases two and three) and a query. A procedure that elicited complex replies would invite trouble with sentences beyond the translator's ken. Instead, the signs of assent and dissent are relatively clear cut; as Quine has said, "The one that is more serene is the better candidate for 'Yes'." [26]

Informants have been provisionally defined as any competent speakers of the model-language, those who are disposed to describe case conditions in the terms of that model. Linguistic theories of translation can assume ideally competent speakers but, unfortunately, practical translation strategies cannot. Instead, we would have to abide by the testimony of individuals generally regarded as spokespersons for that model, or better yet a number of such individuals. But two further problems then intrude. First, a spokesperson for a model may take a more radical, and therefore less readily translatable, attitude than those who regard themselves as followers of these advocates. Szasz and Skinner are two who seem for various reasons, to play this advocacy role. Second, there is the more subtle problem that persons of apparently equal competence may disagree about the applicability of a certain, say, predicate in the model-language to a representation hypothesized to be in its secondary extension.

We could deal with the first problem by deciding beforehand whether we will take as informants for a model its public advocates or rather its regular practitioners in the field. We might speculate that, other things being equal, the advocates are more likely to provide information that restricts conditions of translation to a narrow base, relative to an informant class of regular practitioners. At least we should be able to tell beforehand which class is which and choose our informants according to our purposes. For instance, if we wish to end up with a very conservative account of translation conditions we are likely to choose the class of advocates for informants.

As to the second problem, disagreements among competent informants for the same model will have to be judged as indicative of regions of uncertainty within the model. In natural languages also there are varied applications of certain expressions that may even be inconsistent and so are wisely avoided for purposes of translation. Representations about which there is frequent disagreement, if that disagreement cannot be traced to uncontrolled variables in experimental conditions, will simply have to be abandoned. One supposes that this will not be a severe problem in the long term, however recurrent and frustrating for the translator, because expressions in a model must have a range of clear representations in their secondary extensions or it would seem that the integrity of the identity of that model is in doubt.

These are problems having to do with what we might call the character of the informant pool; at least they can be handled somewhat self-consciously by the translator. In a broad sense, though, many of the problems surveyed in Chapter 2, which in several cases were far more intractable than these, are also relevant to working with any informant for the purpose of translation. It would be misleading to claim, then, that all the complexities concerning the query-assent process are so easily resolved or even so readily identifiable.

Precursors to Extensional Translation

There are times that those who use a certain vocabulary attempt to communicate with users of another vocabulary. Often, too, this piecemeal translating has an extensional cast, as the referents of the expressions are focused upon by the protagonists in search of common ground. Besides the deliberate nature of our formal strategies for translation, the major difference between these customary exchanges and our extensional translation is that we concentrate on depictions or the *secondary* extension of relevant expressions as focal grounds for translation. For the formal translator it is important not to beg ontological questions and also to be able to manipulate the informants' environment occasionally; so secondary extensions are concentrated upon. However, much important material from this informal and unself-conscious extensional translation can be gathered by the extensional translator as clues for his own investigations. Furthermore, since this chapter has been so elliptical with regard to the models of mental illness themselves, this will give us an opportunity to re-introduce some particulars. It should be recalled, however, that extensional translation itself is a process of work with depictive representations and informants, so only the results of extensional translation and a description of the process can be given on paper.

"Ersatz" extensional translation takes two general forms, the results of which can benefit the translator in preparing for the project. The first has to do with the way clinicians representing diverse models manage to talk to one another in context. Alan A. Stone, in his presidential address to the American Psyhicatric Association, states that the medical model has "provided clinical coherence if not conceptual clarity."[27] It would be most helpful to know how this coherence has been negotiated linguistically, which may in turn contribute to conceptual clarity; such information would be invaluable to the extensional translator. An anthropologist or sociologist could investigate the manner in which, say, a team of psychiatrists who identify themselves as proponents of differing models actually talk to each other about their cases, especially in conferences. It might be hypothesized, based on several suggestions the present authors have received, that in day-to-day clinical contexts the burden of translation falls to the nursing staff, who are themselves trained in a kind of primitive "behaviorese." This then becomes the implicit source language by means of which the psychoanalyst, medical modelist, full-fledged behaviorist, and all the rest must generate a translation. Short of this sort of study the extensional translator, as part of the project preparation, may make observations concerning whatever patterns seem to hold.

We can take a concrete example of how an extensional translator could further intervene by selecting a particular condition for interpretation according to various models.[28] As a result of such an analysis, it should be more obvious what sorts of depictions will be most suitable as cross-model representations, and in general how the translation ought to go. This approach is analogous to that of a field anthropologist who takes a single site important to two language communities and gets hints for translation from the descriptions commonly applied by each community. But this falls short of our preference for conceptual interlinguistic negotiations.

Let us say the translator is interested in the behavioral and medical models, with the latter as the source language. The condition chosen as a focus to garner preliminary clues to translation is called "spontaneous anxiety" or "panic with agoraphobia" in the source language, leading to avoidance of particular places associated with the panic attacks, subsequent restriction of activities, and finally becoming housebound. Further characterization in the source language runs along these lines: "Echocardiogram shows mitral valve prolapse (MVP), a malfunction seemingly linked to spontaneous panic attacks in some cases; should react to application of imipramine."[29]

Let us further suppose that the translator finds the following a typical description in the host behavioral model of patients to whom the medical modelist applies the above characterization: "As one learns what is associated with paralytic behavior, such as heart pounding, unchanging physical posture, etc., one learns how to be helpless. This is a way to avoid dealing with certain situations, and in effect the patient tells himself to learn helplessness so as to achieve this sort of avoidance." Clearly this would not count for us as a translation into the host language, for much tracing of particular expressions needs to be done. But the translator can thus gain some sense of what to look for in a depiction, such as whether the host admits the same features of the patient's activities as relevant to diagnosis, whether "imipramine-responsive" applies in the same instances that "unlearning helplessness" applies, whether there are some typical moments in the depiction of "MVP leading to agoraphobia" that are also identifiable as relevant situations inducing panic behavior," and so on.

Philosophically, the rationale for paying attention to such cases, and to extensional translation generally, whether ersatz or not, is that which cuts against the damage allegedly done by IT. As Scheffler has pointed out,[30] and as Hilary Putnam has emphasized,[31] comparability is not dependent upon common meanings but upon having sufficiently many terms with the same *reference*. In testing for sameness of reference the extensional translator thus establishes grounds for comparability, where those in turn establish grounds for translatability.

The results of the second sort of ersatz extensional translation appear now and then in professional journals as attempts to reconcile diverse viewpoints. One initial difficulty with this literature for our purposes is that it is not always easy to tell when the reconciliation applies to models or less broad conceptual items. However, there are some rather clear-cut examples that use, at least in part, shared extensions of expressions for ameliorating relations among models.

In one such paper, Wallace Wilkins[32] noted that "factors that precipitate and maintain depression," characterized by behaviorists as the removal of a reinforcer, could be characterized by psychoanalysts as instances of object loss. "In this respect," Wilkins notes, "a reinforcer is an object of gratification; an object of gratification is a reinforcer."[33] Actually, Wilkins implicitly calls attention to the *extensions* of the *terms* "gratification" and "reinforcer" on one hand, and the *essential similarity* of the *concepts* of gratification and reinforcement on the other. First he remarks upon the identity of "subject matter," an extensional consideration, and explains it on the basis of the identical nature of the "concepts", an essentialist consideration, though he might just as well have gone in the opposite direction. The result is a proposal for a "synthesis" of psychoanalytic and behavioristic approaches to depression, since anyway each approach is talking about the same thing in basically the same way but using different terms.

A purer form of ersatz extensional translation, also addressing depression from psychoanalytic and behavioral standpoints, appears in an article by Robert Paul Liberman and David E. Raskin.[34] The authors are behaviorists, their source language, and in the course of their essay they are concerned to use "external situations as concommitants of depression" and as common reference points for behavioral and psychoanalytic characterizations. They cite Freud's "Fragment of an Analysis of a Case of Hysteria" as his version of the way an individual learns how physical symptoms can be used to gain solicitude. Liberman and Raskin also suggest that failure to learn how to attain "reinforcers" can be causally linked with ego regression of the depressive to an "earlier state of helplessness"; presumably, then, the failure to function as an operant with respect to one's environment constitutes behaviorally what is the regression of ego into libido for the psychoanalyst.

Pauline B. Bart,[35] in an attempt to integrate psychiatric and sociological theories of depression, notes that events having to do with loss are assumed to result in depression by Freudian, ego-psychological, and existential explanations: "Loss of an ambivalently loved person in the first case, loss of goal in the second case, and loss of meaning in the third."[36] Bart suggests that the loss of a person or a goal may result in the loss of meaning described by existentialists. What is of interest to us is the fact that the general class of events referred to is the same for all three theoretical explanations, and that Bart uses this fact to relate the ways each explanation describes the nature of becoming depressed. Again there is an ambiguity as to whether the shared *concept* of loss (essentialist) or the tendancy to refer to actual losses (extensional) is the ground for relating the explanations.

These, then, constitute two sorts of approach to relating diverse viewpoints that turn on considerations friendly to the extensionalist, while not fulfilling all desiderata. We do not ordinarily think of these efforts as translations, but in our sense of the word they have such earmarks. But, again, they are only aids to extensional translation; that they are familiar parts of the scientific literature helps us to realize that the overall form of translating by common extensions is not as alien as it might seem.

The Limits to Extensional Translation

Given pragmatic grounds governing translation that we have already considered, in combination with a well-confirmed set of representations in the overlap, what can the extensional translator reasonably claim to have achieved? In the case of "Aphrodite" and "Venus" the translator could adopt the rule that "'Aphrodite' in the language of Greek mythology translates into 'Venus' in the language of Roman mythology." This rule is supported by a specifiable minimum degree of paratopicality even though the translator knows there will be instances in which the rule does not hold, or in which the translation is forced at best. After all, some Aphrodite-depictions are not Venus-depictions: "'Aphrodite' translates 'Venus'" does not entail "'Aphrodite' means 'Venus'." Thus we make no claim that a theory of meaning falls out of a translation strategy,[37] just as we do not claim that our translation strategy is dictated by a particular theory of meaning, although it is suggested by one.

The claim sentences in our example above, or their significant components, may also turn out to be translatable without any hint that one "gives the meaning of" the other. Indeed, the limited paratopicality or parathematicality one can reasonably expect to show between these sentences eliminates any pretensions we might have to assert that one claim sentence "gives the meaning of" the other. However, by means of secondary extensions we can satisfy ourselves that one claim sentence satisfies *enough* of the applicability conditions of the other claim sentence to justify a rule of translatability supplemented further by the restrictions of the pattern of conditions set forth by the depictive representations in the overlap.

In the context of justification our above hypothetical translation of a source claim sentence can be broken down into components which are paratopical with the components of a host claim sentence. In the context of discovery the markers in the source claim sentence serve notice to the translator what aspects of depictions to attend to in selecting expressions in the host language to match with the depicted components of the source claim sentence for paratopicality.

Of course, the translator is not acting in a vacuum when taking one claim sentence and matching it for overlap with another. First, the initial match of significant units like "hypochondraic" and "primary deviant" constitutes an hypothesis of paratopicality based on the translator's prior knowledge of each model-language, or prior experience with translation. Second, the depictive representations selected for trials as hypothetical parts of the overlap are themselves informed by the results of matching other claim sentences with similar components from the models. In other words, the matching of claim sentences is part of a *process* of translation taken back and forth between the models in question and among various significant units from each model-language.

The suggested translation above for the claim sentence about hypochondria does not give the meaning of the other even hyperbolically. But this claim sentence will be applicable by a social modelist for a specifiable range of applicability conditions. As in any translation some connotations will not be captured by the host language, or at least not efficiently. "Unsatisfied connotations" is elliptical to the extensional translator for those applicability conditions that one claim sentence does not meet, as in this case the social model claim sentence does not meet the conditions of chemical imbalance-depictions, for those are not representations in its secondary extension. Were the translator to work from the social model claim sentence to a medical model claim sentence, it is reasonable to suppose that the latter would fail to meet some of the former's applicability conditions, though as in natural language translation the result of working in the opposite direction should be largely the same.

It is helpful to remember more generally what a bilingual turned translator wants to accomplish. As we noted in Chapter 2, competence in two languages is a necessary condition, but certainly not an automatic guarantee of competence as a translator between those languages, for in communication within a language nuances important for translation are commonly missed. And grounds for application of an expression in a language are not ordinarily demanded. But the translator is obliged to consider both the details that restrict an otherwise efficient translation and the evidence supporting prescribed translations. Perhaps our discussion of extensional translation renders these clues and justifications for ordinary translation strange by focusing upon them and formalizing them in the unfamiliar garb of secondary extension. Still, they are an implicit phase of the translator's task.

The ingenious translator will vary the use of his apparatus, of course. For example, the translator, a bilingual, may hit upon a depiction that seems to him to exhibit just the attributions of both models to such a case. After testing this initial hunch by the query-assent technique, he may then set out to see which significant units of the claim sentences have the depictions or parts of the depictions in their secondary extensions, and which parts of the picture are in both secondary extensions of the claim sentences' significant units. Or he might use the depiction to help him isolate descriptions in the language of either model, and thus obtain further depictions of these descriptions for testing hypothesized overlaps at these more elementary levels of reference.

Concluding Remarks

Extensional semantic theory, including Goodman's theory of reference, provides guidelines for what we have called extensional translation but, as we have emphasized, it is a separate matter how well the theory explains the adequacy of any translation program. We make no pretension to treat this latter question. We have also mentioned that other theories with somewhat different aims make similar suggestions to the translator. Let us briefly illustrate this point with an example.

Neil Wilson's theory of decipherment,[38] distinguishes between primitive predicates and defined predicates. Primitive predicates signify properties such as sense qualities and matter kinds, while defined predicates do not signify properties and are derivative from other words. Taking the example of the English word "iron," it signifies a matter kind by nature, so in primary semantics the lexicographer has "'iron' in English signifies iron," which is not very helpful. Thus the lexicographer must move to secondary semantics and "give us a corpus comprising the essential information about iron."[39] That corpus would list a number of properties associated with instances of iron, in order to provide the individual ignorant of the meaning of "iron" a "sufficient stock of beliefs to qualify him as 'understanding' this word...." Wilson distinguishes between understanding the word and knowing the meaning of the word, for knowing the atomic weight of iron might be helpful in understanding (knowing how to apply) the word but is unnecessary for knowing the meaning of "iron."

Wilson's strategy interestingly cuts between essentialist and extensional translation, as he recommends compiling a corpus listing a number of essential properties. The extensional translator takes "essential properties" to mean a set of "x-representations consistently assented to by any competent informant under appropriate observational conditions." An English-speaking informant and an informant from another language would find a certain overlap of iron-representations that would constitute the paratopicality of the word for iron in each language.

Wilson's theory of decipherment points us in a direction similar to that indicated by an extensional semantic theory, and actually is directed toward lexicographic matters explicitly. However, it does not introduce the prospect that depictions of purported referents might be used as well as descriptions. For our purposes depictions are well worth including, since we could not test the descriptive corpus by seeking the assent of a native speaker of the source language, as the expressions of the corpus are couched in the terms of the host language.

Notes

1. Quine, *Logical Relativity and Other Essays*, p. 27.

2. Since we are more interested in a translation strategy than in a semantic theory, we can and must be selective in our presentation of the latter topic, though its general review is helpful as an introduction to the guidelines of extensional translation. Our reliance upon the accounts of extensionalism in the theory of reference offered by Nelson Goodman and Rolf A. Eberle will therefore be profound but incomplete, as we do not attempt to reproduce all the considerations they have adduced on this topic. Also, when we remark upon the notion of reference in

various contexts it is as explicated extensionally, as against other theories of reference such as the causal approach described by Putnam and others in recent literature.

3. It is another question whether practical guidelines or principles of actual translation can be "inconsistent" with a semantic theory, for adequate translation is adequate translation even if it has been arrived at by a series of lucky guesses.

4. Donald Davidson, "Truth and Meaning," *Synthese* 17, (1967): 304–323.

5. Ruth M. Kempson, *Semantic Theory* (Cambridge: Cambridge University Press, 1977), p. 26.

6. "Two Dogmas of Empiricism," *From A Logical Point of View*.

7. Analytic truth, or analyticity, is taken by some philosophers to be characteristic of necessarily true sentences, i.e. sentences true by virtue of their meaning along and independent of empirical claims as expressed in synthetically true sentences.

8. The uninteresting exception to this is "bachelor that is not an unmarried man," but more on this later.

9. See Nelson Goodman, "About," *Problems and Projects* (Indianapolis: Bobbs-Merrill, 1953).

10. This leaves open the possibility that the latter is compatible with speech act semantics, but that is not a matter we can pursue.

11. See Kempson, *Semantic Theory*, pp. 41–43, for a discussion of this problem in truth-based semantics.

12. Rolf A. Eberle, "Goodman on Likeness and Difference of Meaning," *Erkenntnis* 12, (1978), p. 3.

13. Rolf A. Eberle, "Semantic Analysis Without Reference to Abstract Entities," *The Monist* 61, (1978): 365–383.

14. Jerrold Katz, *Semantic Theory* (New York: Harper & Row, 1974), pp. 235–237.

15. The treatment in the text applies mainly to count nouns, that is, nouns that take the articles "the" or "a," and predicates. It is possible to refine further this line of treatment so that we can see how to use secondary extensions in translating other parts of sentences and whole sentences. The following summary of Eberle's account is noted as a matter of record. It includes means for treating descriptions as well as depictions, though for technical reasons to be discussed later the extensional translator trades only in depictions in translating between models; both can be used when refining understanding of the extensions of expressions within a model. For Eberle's account see "Semantic Analysis Without Reference to Abstract Entities," pp. 366–368.

   Adjectives. "Intelligent" can be treated like a count noun, with its secondary extension including depictions or descriptions of intelligent people, for example.

   Intransitive verbs. Secondary extension includes depictions or descriptions of Tom laughing for instance.

   Names. A picture of Tom laughing is also a picture of Tom, and so is also a part of the secondary extension of that name.

   Sentences of subject-predicate form. We can say that *given an object x* that object is in the extension of its predicate, so that "Tom laughs" has in its secondary extension pictures of Tom laughing only if "Tom" is in the secondary extension of "laughs." In other words, we want the Tom laughs-representations and not just the conjunction of Tom-representations and laughs-representations.

   Transitive verbs and sentences of relational form. Four kinds of extensions are used in the case of a sentence containing a verb such as "kisses":

   1. The primary and secondary extensions of "kisses," comprising all individuals which are either kissers or kissed or all kisser-representations;

   2. For some arbitrary individual x the primary and secondary extensions of "kisses" *given x in the first position*, comprising all individuals x kisses or all representations of kisses given by what x represents;

   3. For any individual y extensions of "kisses" *given y in the second position* comprising kissers

of y or all representations of how what y represents is kissed;

4. For given objects x and y the extensions of "kisses" *given x in the first and y in the second position* the primary extension comprises all and only cases of x kissing y, or secondary extensions showing how what x represents kisses what y represents.

Since our purpose is not to formulate a complete semantic theory we need not take responsibility for further elaboration of the details of this system, particularly as regards the formal interpretation of a fully developed extensional object language. Again, our interest in extensional semantics is limited to ascertaining guidelines for extensional translation. The above remarks serve only to suggest the parameters for such a project, supporting the prospect that complex sentences can be treated under this approach.

16. *Ibid.*, p. 369.

17. For all we know, prior to translation "goddess of love" in Roman mythology may have a virgin in its extension, and in Greek mythology a prostitute.

18. In labeling theory the actual or alleged behavior that is labeled deviant is termed "primary deviance," whereas the deviant career that results from the labeling is called "secondary deviance."

19. Quine, *Word and Object*, p. 69.

20. Willard V. Quine, *The Roots of Reference* (LaSalle, Illinois: Open Court, 1974), p. 14 ff.

21. Noam Chomsky, *Reflections on Language* (New York: Random House, 1972), p. 192.

22. Quine, *Word and Object*, pp. 271–272.

23. Quine, *Ontological Relativity and Other Essays*, p. 45.

24. *Ibid.*, p. 35.

25. Eugene A. Nida, *Language Structure and Translation* (Stanford: Stanford University Press, 1975), Chapter 6.

26. Quine, *Word and Object*, pp. 29–30.

27. Alan A. Stone, "Presidential Address: Conceptual Ambiguity and Morality in American Psychiatry," *American Journal of Psychiatry* 137:8, (1980): p. 887.

28. For many of the ideas in this section we are indebted to Seymour Perlin, M.D.

29. For a recent study in support of an hypothesis to this effect see Jerry S. Kantor, Charlotte Marker Zitrin, and Steven M. Zeldin, "Mitral Valve Prolapse Syndrome in Agoraphobic Patients," *American Journal of Psychiatry* 137:4, (1980): 467–469.

30. Scheffler, *Science and Subjectivity*.

31. Hilary Putnam, *Mind, Language and Reality* (Cambridge: Cambridge University Press, 1975), p. 281.

32. Wallace Wilkins, "Psychoanalytic and Behavioristic Approaches Toward Depression: A Synthesis?" *American Journal of Psychiatry* 128, (1971): 358–359.

33. *Ibid.*, p. 359.

34. Robert Paul Lieberman and David E. Raskin, "Depression: A Behavioral Formulation," *Archives of General Psychiatry* 24, (1971): 515–523.

35. Paul B. Bart, "The Sociology of Depression," in Paul M. Roman and Harrison M. Truce, eds., *Explorations in Psychiatric Sociology* (Philadelphia: F.A. Davis, 1978).

36. *Ibid.*, p. 142.

37. See J. Wallace, "Logical Form, Meaning, Translation," in F. Guenthner and M. Guenthner-Reutter, eds., *Meaning and Translation* (New York: New York University Press, 1978). Herein is an argument that a translation manual is not a theory of translation.

38. Neil L. Wilson, "Concerning the Translation of Predicates," in *Meaning and Translation*.

39. *Ibid.*, p. 104.

5

Essentialist Translation

We shall be taking essentialism in a fairly standard way, as a view that some attributes of a thing are essential and others accidental. Its essential attributes are those that it must have, necessarily. A brief rehearsal of some aspects of philosophical discussions of essentialism will help to clarify the relation of our essentialist translation strategy to its antecedents, though unlike the philosophical sources it is not proposed as informing semantic theory.

Historical accounts of essentialist doctrines ordinarily begin by citing Aristotle's *Metaphysics*, especially when he says that the essence of a thing constitutes what the thing is.[1] The following passage from W. D. Ross' translation is also often cited.

> The essence of each thing is what is said to be its *propter se* (what it is in virtue of itself). For being you is not being musical, since you are not by your very nature musical. What, then, you are by your very nature is your essence.[2]

Aristotle continues by entertaining some of the difficulties and consequences of this notion, especially the determination of a thing's essence. If the formula of a thing is a definition then the thing has an essence, but this definition is not a mere identity in meaning between a word for a thing and its formula. Rather, the formula is of something "primary; and primary things are those which do not imply the predication of one element in terms of another element."

> Nothing, then, which is not a species of a genus will have an *essence*—only species will have it, for these are thought to imply not merely that the subject participates in the attribute and has it as an affection, or has it by accident... .[3]

A passage in the *Posterior Analytics* (Mure's translation) has it that "[p]redicates not signifying substances which are predicates of a subject not identical with themselves or with a species of themselves are accidental or coincidental; e.g., white is a coincident of man, seeing that man is not identical with white or a species of white, but rather with animal, since man *is* identical with a species of animal."[4] In this tradition a thing changes when it gains or loses properties accidental to it, whereas alteration in the presence or absence of essential properties constitutes that thing's coming into or going out of existence.

In modern philosophy the doctrine has been as often criticized as mentioned. John Locke in *An Essay Concerning Human Understanding* set the pace for the standard criticism in a section entitled "Nothing Essential to Individuals":

> Take but away the abstract ideas by which we sort individuals and rank them under common names, and then the thought of anything essential to any of them instantly vanishes.... So that essential and not essential relate only to our abstract ideas.[5]

According to Locke no one of a thing's properties is any more essential to it than any other; the illusion to the contrary that some of us have is owed to our conventional manner of conceiving and naming these things. Quine[6] has rather offhandedly attacked the distinction between necessary and contingent properties as that "invidious attitude" toward certain ways of "uniquely specifying" an object while "favoring other ways as somehow better revealing the 'essence' of the object."[7]

The doctrine being criticized, supposedly Aristotelian essentialism, is easily confused with another sort of essentialism called "realism," which would hold that universals or properties exist independent of thought.[8] Actually, Locke seems to ascribe to Aristotle this view, but one could be an anti-realist and still believe that things do have essential properties but that they inhere in our thought of these things, as Locke himself sometimes comes to think. Thus Quine objects on the grounds that what properties an object can be conceived as having and as not having depends upon the way we choose to describe the object, but in itself this is not damaging to the essentialist position, not without an argument to the effect that the mode of description is arbitrary.

Indeed, among the more prominent modern essentialists is Edmund Husserl, who is generally considered an idealist, or else a subjectivist. This charge might be rejected in light of Husserl's insistence that his project is to investigate how persons interpret the real and external world, and in light of one of his own studies, in which historical data is given considerable importance.[10] Independent of where one wishes to place Husserl on the idealist-realist continuum, it is he who works out in greatest detail many ways of examining essences. Though we will not concern ourselves with the more controversial moves he makes in the course of his life's work (e.g., the transcendental and phenomenological reductions), we can utilize Husserl's notions of essences, which hold them to be the necessary and immutable complex of characteristics without which the phenomenon cannot be conceived. The essences are not generalities or ideal types, but rather are concrete properties of the phenomenon.[11]

Several philosophers have sought recently to define a version of an essentialism more or less in the Aristotelian tradition. Eli Hirsch, for example, defends the view[12] that "a few of the terms which are true of an object play a quite special role in determining the object's identity, and these terms are, in a sense, necessary to the object's identity."[13] Hirsch preliminarily distinguishes between these "E terms" and "A terms" according to the criterion

> A general term F is an E term if and only if the statement "This F (thing) was (or will be) at place p at time t" logically entails "there was (or will be) an F (thing) at place p at time t"; a general term is an A term if and only if it is not an E term.[14]

In Hirsch's example, "This table was in Chicago in 1960," logically entails, "There was a table in Chicago in 1960," so "table" is an E term. However, "red" is an A term since, "This red thing was in Chicago in 1960," does not logically entail, "There was a red thing in Chicago in 1960," for the thing might have become red after 1960.[15] So E terms must be true for objects throughout their career, while A terms may be true of objects only temporarily.[16]

A different approach to formalizing the notion of essential properties is taken by Daniel Bennett.[17] Bennett distinguishes between necessary properties, such as Socrates' being a man, and natural properties, such as Socrates' being postpubescent; he further distinguishes between *necessary nonphasal properties*, such as Socrates' being a man, and *necessary phasal properties*, such as Socrates' dying. Necessary properties are nonphasal if they are *omnitemporal*, that is, if they are like Socrates' property of being man such that Socrates is always (for as long as he exists) a man, which entails that

$$(\exists x) \left[x \text{ is always (for as long as it exists) a man}\right].$$

Further, Socrates' being a postpubescent more specifically exemplifies a natural *phasal property*. (Necessary properties are natural properties, but the reverse is not always the case.)

Bennett analyzes the schematic proposition that something *a* is necessarily *F*, when *F* is a necessary nonphasal property, as follows:

N. i. There is a time at which *a* is *F*; and
ii. Anything that is over *F* is, for as long as it exists, always *F*; and
iii. ii is a necessary truth.[18]

However, this is not a complete analysis of essential properties, according to Bennett, for essentialist properties are also sortal in that they determine a natural kind. Being a man, as well as being wise and being a philosopher, sorted Socrates from his parts and from the wholes of which he was a part, whereas others of his properties such as being of flesh and blood and being not a dog did not. After a discussion of the part-whole relation and two preliminary analyses of what it is to be a sortal property Bennett offers

S.2. i.   Anything that is *F*, for as long as it is *F*, is sorted up and down by *F*; and

ii.   i is a necessary truth; and

iii.   It is possible that anything that is *F* is, at some time when it is *F*, nonsorted across *F*.[19]

By way of explanation of S.2., a property *F sorts* an individual *a up* at a time *t* when *F* is true of *a* at *t*, but of none of the wholes of which *a* is part at *t*; *F sorts a down* at times *t* when *F* is true of *a* at *t*, but of none of the parts of *a* at *t*. For Socrates being a philosopher sorted him up and down for part of his life; being a man sorted him up and down for all of his life. F could also sort an individual *a across* at a time *t*, when *F* is true of *a* at *t*, but of nothing distinct from *a* at *t*. A property *F nonsorts* an individual *a across* at *t* when *F* is true of *a* at *t*, and of (only) some things distinct from *a* at *t*. Thus S.2.iii is weak enough to allow for the possibility that *F* applies only to one entity; *F* would have to sort up and down but might fail to sort across.[20] For Bennett, then, a "property *F* belonging to an individual *a* is an *essential* property of *a* if and only if the conditions N and S.2 are met."[21]

In this discussion we have touched upon several topics bearing important relations to the notion of essential properties, especially those of analytic or necessary truth, the doctrine of natural kinds, and modal quantification in logic.[22] Without venturing too far afield we have been concerned to describe some systematic articulations of the idea of essential properties and note the historic dimension. Hirsch's treatment can be adapted to our interest in determining the essential properties of a model to show that the adoption of that model logically entails the assumption of certain concepts; and, using Bennett's analysis of S.2 especially, any essential conceptual feature in the model must sort it both up and down, must sort it up from its disciplinary context as well as down from each of its component sentences, but not necessarily across, from other models.

Essentialism can be taken, however, in quite as many ways by translation strategists as can a Rorschach design by any other sort of neurotic, and thus, we will need to specify carefully our usage of essentialism in the translation of models.

Rejected Essences

When we talk of the essences of a physical object we consider its material properties, as the preceding discussion has suggested. In the case of phenomena that are not solely material, we speak of identifying processes, which may or may not involve material properties. Thus, in a preliminary analysis of the essences of prejudice, Glassner[23] has suggested that instrumentality and simplification are essential properties. The conclusion is reached by comparing hundreds of accounts of prejudice, written from different theoretical, methodological, and historical perspectives, and by ascertaining which features are found in all of the accounts and without which prejudice would not be distinguishable from related phenomena.

One could proceed in roughly the same manner in seeking essences of mental illness, by searching through the disparate accounts about the phenomenon in order to derive which properties appear to be necessary and identifying of madness. To do so might aid in construction of a meta-model or metalanguage, but it would not help in translation, since extant models may not discuss essences *per se*, and the essences of madness need not be involved in the essential structure of the models themselves. For essentialist translation one requires instead the essences of the *models* of madness, as we have suggested, but there are many sorts of candidates for recognition as essences of models.

In a sense many if not all translators are essentialists of a kind, because they emphasize in their work what they consider to be the truly significant aspects of texts they are translating. A "literal translator" takes the words and grammar to be the essences of the text and seeks to identify precisely the same words and grammar in the host as in the source. Other translators, notably those concerned with the aesthetic quality of a work, concentrate upon the flow or feeling of the piece. Translators in science will pay special attention to technical terms or to findings and rather less to digressions on the fine points of an experimental protocol.

None of these are essentialist translation strategies in our sense, of course, but rather are translations that favor certain features of texts over others. Essentialist translations are efforts toward foundations of texts or models, not preemptory rulings about such foundations. We begin not with an emphasis on particular aspects of a model, but with techniques for uncovering and utilizing those components without which the text or model could not exist. We might find, for instance, were we essentialist translators of poetry, that meter is essential to a given poem, but this would need to be discovered from working with the particular poem, or with poems as a form, not ruled *a priori* or on the ground that this is what we choose to emphasize about poems.

One might argue, however, that in some areas enough scholarship has been completed so that we do know in advance of new translations which aspects are essential. Of poetry it might be suggested that while meter or rhyme are not important or even present in every poem, the goal to evoke feelings from the reader is always to be found. Or of social scientific models it would appear that efforts after explanation can be identified in every case.

These claims may be true, and lists of such features may be devisable prior to any particular translation. But the types of essential features that appear on such lists would seem to be of little use for actual translation activities. To know the general features of social science models, such as their inclusion of explanations, does little to help us translate a claim sentence from one model to another. Knowing that all models have certain features may identify for us which sorts of items can be translated—e.g., that explanations are translatable in general—but such knowledge does not aid in any obvious way in the translation of actual examples of the feature, such as a particular explanation about something.

The argument might be pushed further, however, in ways that are not so easy to dismiss. The position may be that while our disclaimers are appropriate against deriving essential features by way of commonsense or general scholarship, there are nevertheless pronounced and adequate theories about the production of knowledge, and these permit us to ascertain in advance of particular translations the essential features of discourse to be utilized in translations. For example, we might employ psychological theories in order to identify key features of the models of madness. Althusser's analysis of the young Marx, and Ernest Jones' psychoanalytic interpretations of Freud's work are perhaps the best known instances of such attempts to interpret a theory by way of that theory. Other authors have analyzed specific claims within Freudian theory, by way of psychodynamic analyses of Freud and his family. In addition to such intratheoretic cases, there are intertheoretic analyses, including a recent examination of the personalities of those who subscribe to various models of madness. The study concludes that psychoanalysts tend to be critical, intellectual, not terribly concerned about others, and conscientious, in comparison to practitioners of another method and to a control group of college students.[24]

On the basis of these sorts of applications of social scientific theories one might attempt to determine the truly fundamental aspects of models of madness. Thus, one might identify as essential to Freudian theory aspects such as self-analysis, intellectualism, or even specific psychodynamic conditions for Freud himself, and accomplish translations on the basis of the determinants of these aspects. Although the proposal may sound a bit exotic, it is really only to take the theories seriously, to accept that these theories can explain the structures and processes at work in the construction of human thought.

There are difficulties with this sort of route to essentialist translations, however, even were the strategy worked out far better than in our caricature. First, how should we determine which of the various theories to use for finding the essential components of models? As we noted earlier in the book, nothing like a meta-model, nor even a strategy for arbitrating between models, currently exists. At a more basic level, the application of social scientific theories or traditions in order to identify essential features exemplifies a common form of the genetic fallacy found in psychologies and sociologies of knowledge. Put simply, there is no reason to believe that once the psychology of an author, or the social history of the production of the model, is fully known that the resulting model is known. A variety of psychological and sociological determinants can produce similar products, hence these determinants may be inessential to the actual products, and the nature of the product is not revealed by what produced it. Much as we do not understand the mechanics of how an automobile operates by understanding the psychosocial or material forces that brought about its production, we cannot know how a claim sentence operates in a model by way of the psychology of its author. The error is in mistaking theories of the production of knowledge for theories about the knowledge produced. Apparently Freud's claim sentences about Oedipus complex are responses to the dynamics of his relationships in his family, and he discovered the complex through self-analysis, but the work that the claims do as social scientific explanations can be understood only very incompletely in terms of this. On the basis of a psychosocial analysis of Freud we may be able to say much about why he talks about the complex in the ways he does, or even why some persons find it appealing and others do not, but we will know little or nothing about the place of these claims in a set of interrelated postulates, or about the observations that count as evidence. In short, by applying psychosocial theories about the production of models we reveal some fundamental facts about the psychosocial dimensions of the models but probably nothing essential about the models *qua* models.

There are related problems for a quite different approach to the identification of basic features of models. One might seek the core of a model by way of a kind of structuralist analysis, which seeks the hidden structures that mold and delimit specific forms of thought. To take a famous and relevant example, let us consider the analysis of Oedipus complex by Claude Levi-Strauss.[25]

Levi-Strauss' method is to map out the Greek myth about Oedipus, who unknowingly marries his mother Jocasta, then kills his father and encounters and kills the Sphinx. By charting the events in the myth in terms of similarities and oppositions, he concludes that there are four types of events, as follows:

I	II	III	IV
Kadmos seeks his sister Europa ravished by Zeus.			
		Kadmos kills the dragon.	
	The Spartoi kill each other.		Labdacos (Laios' father) = "lame" (?) Laios (Oedipus' father) = "left-sided"(?).
	Oedipus kills his father Laios.		
		Oedipus kills the sphinx.	
Oedipus marries his mother Jocasta.			
	Eteocles kills his brother Polyneices.		Oedipus = "swollen foot"(?).
Antigone buries her brother Polyneices despite prohibition.			

He proposes that the common property of Column I is the overrating of blood relations, II the underrating of blood relations, III the slaying of monsters, and IV difficulties in walking.

Levi-Strauss argues that the first two columns invert one another, as do the last two; and that the myth is a logical tool that verifies what otherwise would seem a contradictory cosmology, namely, that man is born from earth (autochthonous) and that human beings actually are born from the union of man and woman. The contradiction is overcome by the juxtaposition of contradictory relationships that are both seen to be self-contradictory. On Levi-Strauss' reading, the first column consists of denial of the autochthonous origins of mankind, the second accepts that origin, the third denies it (by demonstrating man's powers over monster), and the fourth accepts it again (trouble in walking is related to birth from the ground).

Of interest to us is Levi-Strauss' proposal that "the myth consists of all its versions," that we are to understand the many versions of Oedipus by way of this structure that Levi-Strauss has uncovered. To support the claim, he points to Freud's Oedipus complex:

A striking example is offered by the fact that our interpretation may take into account, and is certainly applicable to, the Freudian use of the Oedipus myth. Although the Freudian problem has ceased to be that of autochthony *versus* bisexual reproduction, it is still the problem of understanding how *one* can be born from *two*: how is it that we do not have only one procreator, but a mother plus a father? Therefore, not only Sophochles, but Freud himself, should be included among the recorded versions of the Oedipus myth on a par with earlier or seemingly more "authentic" versions.[26]

To the extent that Levi-Strauss is correct in this claim we have our first viable ground for identifying preemptory fundamental features of models. If one can identify the deep structure within which specific forms (i.e., models and claims) arise, and if these structures in any way affect the shape that the forms can take (i.e., if they *structure* the forms), we know a good deal about what is fundamental to a model or a claim.[27] Unfortunately, Levi-Strauss' analysis does not permit such a grounding, both in light of criticisms of the analysis itself, and in consideration of more general limits of this kind of structuralist analysis for translation of models.

Levi-Strauss has been criticized for taking an interpretation which is at once undemonstrated and idiosyncratic. For instance, it is only with great effort that one interprets the event of Antigone burying her brother as an overrating of blood relations, or the Spartoi killing one another as an underrating, and one must take on faith that this really is the deep structure.[28] Indeed, Antigone's burial of her brother in defiance of Kreon's edict would seem to be a simple affirmation of ordinary kinship obligations.[29]

Even if Levi-Strauss' analysis is correct, however, his application to Freud's use of the Oedipus myth remains more confusing for the translator than it is enlightening. A source of the problem was noted by Octavio Paz in his suggested distinction between mythical and modern thought: "In myth a logic unfolds which does not confront reality and its coherence is merely formal; in science, the theory must be subjected to the proof of experiment; in philosophy, thought is critical. I admit that myth is logical, but I do not see how it can be knowledge."[30] On structuralism's own grounds, we might say that Levi-Strauss' analysis of Freud neglects to put the structure of the myth within its new system, that of scientific modeling. Had he done so, perhaps he would not be susceptible to the criticism that Paz raises and might instead discuss the unfolding of the logic of the myth. Indeed, there is evidence from within Freud's work that such an interpretation might be possible and productive. In the Greek case, reparation for the parricide is made by the incest, and the autochthony is amended by killing the monster. Freud claimed that for the boy the Oedipus complex is destroyed by the castration complex, in the girl by the desire to receive a child from her father as a gift.[31] He also held that the complex is resolved or transformed through identification with the parent of the same sex and temporary renunciation of the other parent. One might work out an argument that these are modern, in-the-world actions that parallel the myth's resolution.

The force of Paz's critique would not be diminished by way of this move, however, at least for translators. To reveal that Freud's theory works out to be within the structural lines of the myth does not help us to understand a claim sentence about Oedipus complex within a social scientific model, because the reading and usage of the myth is different in the model than in its traditional context. The myth has not only a structure, but is a narrative: It tells a story. That story can be "read" in a variety of ways, and these readings have much to do with the derivative products built upon the myth. Much as the underrating of blood relations may be, and in fact, is, symbolized in different ways in different versions of the myth cross-culturally, and those ways of symbolizing must be integral parts of the translation from natural language to natural language, the local content of Freud's usage of the myth is important for translating from model to model. It is how Freud "reads" and builds the myth that principally shapes the claims he makes about the Oedipus complex, and it is his claims that we are concerned to translate . The local context within which a structure is used may be important.

One might respond that our objection asks more than the structuralist can provide, given that within the structuralist movement it is accepted that specific meanings cannot be predicted on the basis of structures, but that by knowledge of the generative features one knows broadly what to expect and much of what will not be found. Unfortunately, a fundamental element in Levi-Strauss' ontology forces the translator to be more suspicious than the retort recommends. Levi-Strauss seeks in his analyses of myths a deep seated polarization. He expects myths to consist in a structure of binary oppositions, and in the analysis of Oedipus this is a major ground for his conclusions. Not all thinkers work in binary oppositions, however, and Freud is a case in point.

Triads (most notably: id, ego, superego) tend to dominate in his worldview, including his interpretations of the Oedipus complex. Despite Levi-Strauss' claim, Freud is not considering "how one can be born from two," but rather the love and sexual relations in a triangle of mother, father, and child.[32] The resolutions noted above are viewed in psychodynamic theory not as solutions to binary opposition, but as methods whereby a destructive triangular process is averted.[33]

Again, it may be only that Levi-Strauss' analysis is incomplete or flawed, and that this family dynamic really is somewhere in the structure of the myth. Another prominent French structuralist, Jacques Lacan, interprets the Oedipus myth in terms of language, claiming that the crisis arises from the child's understanding of the sexual rules found in the culture's words for family units. Aspects like the way in which a father passes down his name to his children become the primary dimensions of the Oedipus condition, and the Oedipus unit consists of the "Father-Mother-Me" equation. On Lacan's reading, the crisis is one of a triad: Prior to the Oedipal stage the child was in a twosome or fusional relationship with the mother, based on their symbolic discourse; then the father enters the world of communication of the child and creates a crisis by mediating between the one-to-one relationship. The Oedipal crisis ends when the child accepts his or her prescribed place in the family and in the language-society.[34]

An especially detailed structuralist analysis of the myth in terms of family relations is Terence Turner's,[35] which concludes that threesomes are "the central symbol of the myth" and that "the central theme of the Oedipus story is the mutual interdependence of kinship relations and relations between non-kinsmen in the context of intergenerational relations." Turner's work consists of a dialectical structuralist method not outside standard structuralist protocol. Yet he concludes that Freud built his Oedipus complex claims upon a *mis*reading of the text. Rather than seeing a conflict between father and son, which is focused on patrilineal succession, as the primary factor in bringing about Oedipus' incestuous marriage, Freud is said to interpret in just the opposing way: That Oedipus' incestuous desire for his mother produces the conflict with his father.

Since multiple readings are so prevalent, and even misreadings are possible, this kind of structuralist analysis would not seem to be a route to fundamental units of models. Models are built at least as significantly upon readings as upon structures.[36]

Techniques for Essentialist Translation

To put the matter another way, these seemingly essentialist strategies err by seeking essences that are too wide for the needs of translation. Generalization to models of psychosocial theories or of a culture's or myth's deep structures, may reveal essences of models or ways of talking in general, or even of a particular sort of model, but not of a specific individual model. "Essence," George Santayana noted, "is just that character which any existence wears in so far as it remains identical with itself and so long as it does so." [37]

The types of essences sought for translation purposes are those involved in claim-making, since it is claims that we wish to translate (as argued in Chapter 2). There would appear to be two sorts of essences involved in claims: (1) concepts, and (2) grounds for arguments. The essential concepts of a model are those from which other concepts are developed or upon which other concepts are built. Some would call these essential concepts "primitives," [38] but we dare not grant them this stature, since in the models of madness there is not formal development of defined terms logically from primitives, as there is, say, in physics, where nearly all terms are built up from mass, length, and time. [39] Nevertheless, we do find that only a limited number of all concepts in a model are used in the development of other concepts, and for essentialist translation we seek to identify these. The second sort of essence of models, the grounds for arguments, also turns out to be only a few of the arguments in a model. If models did not have characteristic arguments that they use in making their various claims, we would hardly be able to distinguish one model from another. Even at the commonsense level we can imagine, for instance, that something like mentalism is an essential ground for arguments that distinguishes psychoanalytic models from behaviorist models.

In order to identify the essences of models we turn to a couple of properties of models that exhibit with special clarity what is essential and inessential to models. Despite a common misunderstanding of essentialism as *a priori* rather than empirical, [40] it is only through examination of the models themselves that we reach essentialist conclusions. First, by examining the definitions that models offer, we look at what might be called *ethnoessentialist* accounts, because in their definitions modelers present their views of what, in fundamental terms, a phenomenon really is. Second, models develop, and in their development one can often identify which grounds for claim making are used because they are needed, and which are responses to temporary circumstances within the history of the model or its relations to other models.

Definitional analyses offer clues about the fundamental concepts of the model, whereas developmental analyses suggest the grounds for claim-making (Figure 9).

Definitional Analysis

In accomplishing the second step in translation—development of a detailed diagram of the claim sentence in the source model—a viable place for the essentialist to turn is to definitions of key terms in both models. A request for the essence of something is a request for a definition, or for some of the defining characteristics, of that thing. [41] At least in social scientific discourse, the definitions that modelers and researchers offer tend to consist of the

Properties suggesting essences of specific models	General properties of models	
	Basic concepts	Grounds for claim making
Definitions	x	
Development		x

Figure 9

briefest explanation they can construct for the phenomenon. They include in their definitions those characteristics and processes without which, on the model's view, the phenomenon would not be itself. Although definitions may be proposed carelessly or otherwise inadequately, to a greater extent than do other statements within a modeler's works, definitions include what the modelers themselves consider essential to the phenomenon.

Aristotle's famous distinction between nominal definitions (what the name of a thing signifies) and real definitions (what something actually is) collapses for the essentialist translator, though only for strategic purposes. The essentialist translator will typically find modelers purporting to have real definitions,[42] but in light of differences between definitions within various models, and in the absence of a meta-model, the translator does not know whether any particular definition is real or nominal. On Aristotle's view both types of definition suggest essences.[43] Real definitions signify essences directly, nominal indirectly. Nominal definitions identify a phenomenon by reference to examples of the phenomenon, by pointing to features of the phenomenon, and by listing conditions for membership as a case of the phenomenon. There are two sorts of nominal definition according to Aristotle. The first is exemplified by a definition of thunder, "Thunder is a certain noise in the clouds." This does not reveal what thunder is but rather a noise-type that we identify as thunder. Nevertheless, this nominal definition entails essence claims, namely, that thunder is a phenomenon whose members have the specified noise-type as essence. The second variety of nominal definition is exemplified by a definition of eclipse as "the failure of the full moon to cast shadows when nothing visible is in the way." Since eclipses take place on cloudy days, this definition does not give a necessary feature of eclipses. It does suggest, however, an essence of eclipses, i.e., it tells us that under familiar circumstances (a clear sky) the full moon will fail to cast a shadow. Thus, the definition points out that something is an eclipse that has the essence of these familiar cases.[44]

For Aristotle, nominal definitions point us in the direction of essences, which our scientific inquiries must then investigate. In social science models we find definitions that may or may not be guideposts to true essences, but which either claim to name actual essences and causes ("delusion: a false belief, born of morbidity"[45]) and hence to be real definitions, or which identify what the concept signifies in the model ("fright is the name of the condition to which one is reduced if one encounters a danger without being prepared for it"[46]) and hence to be a nominal definition. We do not seek in an essentialist translation to uncover essences of phenomena, but rather of models, and for us all definitions in models must be treated as if they required the additional work that Aristotle considered necessary only with nominal definitions. For Aristotle, the work of science was to develop real definitions, and nominal definitions necessitated a search to uncover the disguised essences of the phenomenon: e.g., what about the absence of a shadow on a clear evening reveals the essences of eclipse? The essentialist translator will ask related questions of purported nominal definitions: e.g., does anything about unpreparedness reveal the essences of Freudian theory as applied to fright? But for purported real definitions the translator must also inquire beyond the given: e.g., what about false belief involves the essences of the psychoanalytic model? In short, with purported nominal definitions the translator seeks to discover not only how, but whether, the definition suggests essential features of the model; whereas with purported real definitions the translator seeks to discover how the definition is related to essential features of the model.

The actual analysis to seek essences from definitions consists of examination of texts from the model in order to uncover how the definition is developed from the basic concepts of the model. Often this will entail a tracing backward of a string of concepts. The procedure is built upon the everyday strategy that one might adopt in trying to get at the root of a word in a natural language. If we want to know what "happy" means in English we take out a dictionary and look up the word. Here we find the primary definition is "favored by circumstances; lucky; fortunate."[47] If we look up these words we find more words: advantages, privileged, good luck, fortunate, lucky, favorable, auspicious. In short, we come across three new words and repeats of some we had already found. In looking up the three new words we find: favorable positions, superiority, favorable or beneficial circumstances, advantage, favor, good omen, favorable, propitious. This process could continue with the new words thus derived, but eventually the point becomes clear: we keep finding key words, in this case "favorable" (or its root, "favor"), and perhaps "lucky."

To analyse the purported real definition for delusions, as noted above, one consults not only psychoanalytic dictionaries but also other texts in which "false beliefs" and "morbidity" are discussed. In so doing, the following string emerges: reality testing, ego versus non-ego relations, unconscious versus conscious, defences, distinctions from id and super-ego, repression, ego-threatening impulses, object-relations, ego, unconscious, etc. In short, unconscious and ego each appear several times and where false beliefs and morbidity are discussed as conjoined, these are often brought up. Though a full analysis of this sort might reveal something different, this cursory look gives us a good indication that unconscious and ego are essential concepts of the psychoanalytic model, upon which the concept of delusion is built. Of course, in an actual translation we verify this by looking at much more than the definition of a single term. If unconscious and ego are essential concepts, we will come across them in definitional analyses of other terms as well, and they will be involved in the grounds for claim making that we find through developmental analyses.

The results of definitional analysis are included in the diagram of the claim sentence (along with the results from the developmental analyses as proposed below). Usually definitional analysis will produce material for diagramming the nouns in a claim sentence. If, for instance, we were diagramming a psychoanalytic claim about delusions, and had determined that the unconscious is essential to psychoanalyatic theory, "delusion" in the sentence might be diagrammed to show the connections between morbidity and the unconscious as applied to this phenomenon. Perhaps the diagram fragment would look like Figure 10.

We will discuss below how to move from diagrams of the source claim sentence to development of the claim in the host model, but suggestions for such moves are evident even in this diagram fragment. For instance, we can imagine some ways to start translating into various social models on the basis of the items "on others" and "symbolized," terms whose replicas appear in various ways in social models as well. Or movement to behaviorist models might be facilitated by way of "rejected impulses."

Developmental Analysis

Definitions of items in the claim sentence present the translator with a compressed version of the way of talking in the source model about the topics at hand and thereby aid in the essentialist translator's basic goal of interpreting the particular claim as an instance of the model's general claims. Definitional analysis can permit at most, however, only identification of core *concepts* involved in modelers' claim-making. The most productive tool for developing essentialist diagrams, because it is the most far reaching, is likely to be analysis of the model's development, which suggests its essential *grounds* for claim-making.

The way in which the model developed will have a great deal to do with how it operates. A few pages back we argued against inappropriate extensions of this insight, namely those that confuse the production of a model with the truth or operation of the model at present, and those that suppose there is a metapsychosocial theory by which we can analyze models on the basis of how they were produced. Now we wish to rescue the developmental analysis, to use it in a rather contrasting way. By examining the history of a model we can separate its bases for making claims from the way it happens to talk as a result of its history.

Suppose we are translating a claim sentence from Emile Durkheim's model of suicide: "Suicide rates can be explained only with societal level data, not on

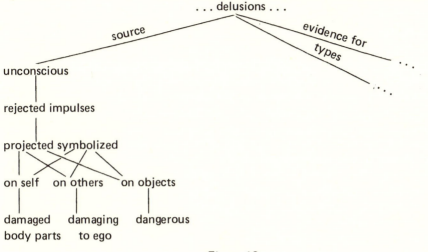

Figure 10

the basis of individuals or biology, because the moral states of society are what cause suicide."[48] The task of translating into nearly any psychological model would appear difficult, at least if one seeks a statement more appealing to the host modeler than "you are not competent to study suicide." By looking at the development of Durkheim's work, however, we begin to avert this difficulty. As a founder of the new discipline of sociology Durkheim was in a battle for legitimacy. He needed to demonstrate that sociology could explain phenomena in ways as good or better than did the extant disciplines, and suicide was the acid test, since it seemed to be "an individual action affecting the individual only (and to) depend exclusively on individual factors, thus belonging to psychology alone."[49] He revealed his personal stakes when he declared:

> Since the system of accepted ideas must be modified to make room for the new order of things and to establish new concepts, men's minds resist through mere inertia. Yet this understanding must be reached. If there is such a science as sociology, it can only be the study of a world hitherto unknown, different from those explored by other sciences.[50]

It turns out upon analysis that Durkheim's belligerence about societal level explanations is inessential to his claims. It is true enough that Durkheim's is a sociological model of suicide. Yet, in light of his more general social scientific theory, and his complete statements of position in *Suicide*, we must not interpret his emphasis as a contention that persons are brought passively or mechanically to suicide by the invisible power of Society, even though he compares the forces of society to those of cosmic and physicochemical forces.[51] Rather, his concern is with the moral order or bonding that society sets up, just as it had been in his earlier works on education, the family, and the division of labor. In *Suicide* Durkheim is arguing that his research reveals three specific forms of dissolution of social bonds, or three relatively uncommon relationships between persons and their groups, which obviate the ability of the group to provide reasons for living or sanctions against self-destructive behaviors. In altruistic suicide persons are too tightly connected to the group and take their lives because they can no longer benefit the group except by dying. In egoistic suicide persons are too loosely connected to the group, so that they no longer see any justification for living. Finally, in anomic suicide, the group is unable to regulate the persons because within society there is an absence of clear rules. During the same period that he developed this analysis, Durkheim proposed the guiding notions in other works. In his discussions of moral education Durkheim considered the nature and importance of persons' bonds to social groups (and to society more generally), and thus set the stage for introducing his description of the first two forms of suicide. In these lectures and writing he also discussed the importance of social regulation; anomie is named in *Division of Labor*, which was published four years prior to *Suicide* but three years after he lectured on the topic of suicide at Bordeaux.

Durkheim's belligerent refusal to reduce suicide to an individual, psychological, or chemical phenomenon may be essential to his project of establishing sociology as an independent discipline, but not to his explanatory claims about suicide. On the other hand, his non-reductionist (i.e., societal) focus surely is essential, but it must be specified in terms of his overall theory as applied to a particular claim sentence. When this is done, one finds that what is really at stake *for the Durkheimian model* is the relationship of social bonds to suicide. One might say that the first part of the claim sentence (suicide rates can be explained only with societal level data) becomes subservient to the second part (the moral states of society are what cause suicide) once both are understood in an essentialist manner. This is suggested by the fact that the Durkheimian model can do quite well at explanation without the aggressive sociologizing: Remove the attacks on psychology and one still has the Durkheimian explanation of suicide. In contrast, remove the notions of social bonds or moral order and the explanation makes no sense. Egoistic, altruistic, and anomic suicide become nonsense phrases.

A careful examination of *Suicide* reveals, in addition, some positive evidence for the inessentiality of anti-psychology in Durkheim's model. In places he puts forth notions that depend upon the psychological level. In discussing marriage and suicide, for instance, Durkheim talks of neurasthenia as "the organic-psychic temperament most predisposing man to kill himself." Of course, he goes on to describe neurasthenia as conditioned by society: "Now today neurasthenia is rather considered a mark of distinction than a weakness. In our refined societies, enamoured of things intellectual, nervous members constitute almost nobility."[52] It would be wrong to say that Durkheim resorts to psychological explanation (as some critics have argued), but correct to identify his usage of the psychological level as entwined in his explanation. As a result, one begins to see hints of translation possibilities to psychological models, such as to Freud, who discusses neurasthenia and its products, and even claims that civilization is responsible for the spread of neurasthenia.[53]

This kind of analysis of a claim sentence in light of the development of the model that produced it, once crafted within the context of an actual translation, can be a valuable aid in preparation of a diagram of that claim sentence for purposes of essentialist translation. In the present example, we would thus avoid the *a priori* untranslatability that results from the source model denying the host's ontology, by eliminating from the claim any aspect of the denial that does not accomplish some explanatory or descriptive work for the source; and yet we remain faithful to the source's ontology (Durkheim's claim is never made psychological or less sociological). At the same time, the translator becomes aware of the centrality of "moral states of society" to the diagram, and might want to examine in detail Durkheim's various discussions of this issue.

There is more to the development of a model than the emerging projects or concerns of its authors, of course, and analysis of these aspects can assist the essentialist translator in separating essential from inessential components of claims. Typically, claims are considered in various ways by proponents of a given model, and through these varied intratheoretic discussions comes some degree of clarity about how the model's principles may and may not apply to the topics at hand. For instance, in translating from Freudian theory to any sociological model—to take the other side of the problem we were just considering—a basic difficulty results from Freud's emphasis on organism- and psychological-level explanations and the great determinism asserted for early childhood development, all of which would seem to exclude precisely those societal level issues of importance to the sociologist. On these grounds Freudian theory has been intentionally ignored or rejected in much sociological work on mental illness.[54]

In the case of Freud's own work we need not go beyond the sort of analysis of an author's projects we have been proposing above, to see the inessentiality of a tendency in places for Freud to talk as if only organic, psychological, or early circumstances enter into his explanations. Freud's background was in the natural sciences through medicine, and it was not until the middle of his life that he broke with a purely neurological practice and research, and then only because he was impressed by the phenomenon of hysteria (seen as a neurological event), and by the fortuitous application by Charcot of hypnotism in the study and treatment of the disorder. By confrontation with the shortcomings of hypnotic method and a fascination for the attachment of the patient to the therapist, which he would later term *transference*, he gradually developed the method of free association, a concern with catharsis and eventually full flown psychoanalysis (ten years after he began with hypnotism, and twelve years after his major contributions to neurology).

In much the same manner that he built "upward" from neurology to the mind, over the following years he developed his thoughts farther and farther toward the social level, at all times constructing them upon his foundational explanans (the unconscious, emphasis on sexuality, defenses, etc.). By the time of his discoveries of libido theory with its developmental phases, he had already started to discuss social-level issues in *The Psychopathology of Everyday Life* and in *Jokes and Their Relation to the Unconscious*. But it was not until a decade later, with *Totem and Taboo*, that he argued in his own words for the importance both of applying his psychological theories at the level of societies and of placing his explanatory principles in their social contexts. In this book the emphasis was clearly on describing various processes within society primarily in terms of the Oedipus conflict. But in subsequent works, notably *Group Psychology* and *Civilization and Its Discontents*, Freud shows clearly that he appreciates the effects of society on individual psychology: The source for many psychological processes he had enunciated in his earlier works is said to be social institutions and groups. Indeed, he actually suggests that the development of the individual takes place amid parallel developmental processes of whole civilizations, talks of "collective neuroses," and calls for "research into the pathology of civilized communities."[55]

In Freud's own view, the central focus of his work had always been culture. In *An Autobiographical Study* he concludes: "My interest, after making a lifelong detour through the natural sciences, medicine and psychotherapy, returned to the cultural problems."[56]

The essentialist translator would seem justified, then, in considering as inessential those not infrequent statements in Freud's work that seem to exclude the social sphere and thereby to make his work untranslatable into social models. As we have indicated, however, the translator may sort out the essential from the inessential in a model not only with this sort of analysis of an author's life projects, but also by extending considerations to developments within the model more generally. If we turn to psychoanalytic theory, we find a number of developments that could facilitate translations to the social models and remain faithful to the essential nature of the psychoanalytic model.

Roger Bastide notes four such developments.[57] First, there has been a longstanding concern with early experiences in the family, which has resulted in numerous discussions of the effects of various family structures and interaction patterns on the Freudian developmental stages and on the structure of personality. In addition, psychoanalysis does not view psychiatric disorders as produced by traumas in childhood in a simple cause-and-effect manner like a ball is caused to move by gravity. Rather the psychoanalytic explanation identifies the reawakening of these traumas by social conditions of the present as crucial in the etiology of neuroses and psychoses. Some analysts, such as Franz Alexander, go so far in the direction of society as to suggest the purely sociological view that it is disturbances in the society that create family disorganization, and this in turn produces disturbances of early childhood relations and mental illness symptoms at various points in the lifespan. Third, psychoanalysis emphasizes the importance of components of the dialogue between patient and therapist or subject and researcher, and hence includes the sociological issues of dyadic relationships. Finally, there have been direct conversions of Freudian principles into quite sociological terms by leading figures within the psychoanalytic movement. Bastide notes the changes brought about by Karen Horney, and there are many names that could be added without controversy, most obviously Erich Fromm, Eric Erikson, and Alfred Adler.

Analyses of these sorts of intratheoretic developments that make the model's claims more easily translatable into certain other models parallel a common move made by natural language translators. When a feature of a source language's culture, or of a source author's style, proves difficult to translate into a given host language, a common move is for the translator to examine whether the feature *must* be carried over in the translation. One may conclude in the negative if the text functions pretty much the same way in the host as in the source when the troublesome feature is eliminated or revised. In Chapter 2 we noted the problem that Lin Shu confronted in translating Dickens into Chinese, that the loquaciousness of Dickens' style would not be acceptable, or at least comfortable, in Chinese. Shu's translations are considered quite effective, and have popularized Dickens, because he was able to abandon the verbiage that Dickens used as a tool for producing ironic humor and yet retain Dicken's characteristic humor within a calm and efficient Chinese wording.

This is not to suggest, however, that inquiry into the development of a model will always reveal that the model's essential structure affords clear grounds for translation. A notable contrary case is where one finds that a model developed primarily *as opposition to* another model or to a group of related models. In these cases, our false fear as applied to Durkheim becomes a real difficulty—the model's message about mental illness cannot stand with its full declarative or explanatory force if one removes contentiousness toward opposing models. Let us consider this special issue of opposition.

Two types of models must be distinguished: Those that developed as oppositions to other models and at times in their history rested upon their opposition but no longer depend upon that opposition in making their claims about mental illness; and the sort just mentioned, which continuously depend upon their belligerence. Labeling theory seems to be an example of the former. Key originators, such as Edwin Lemert, Erving Goffman, and Howard S. Becker, only occasionally have written as if the model is in opposition to psychological theories, and to our knowledge have never rested claims on this opposition. Instead, they often question various assumptions of psychological models, as points of departure for their own research or discussions of their findings. Lemert, for instance, begins his famous paper on paranoia[58] by opposing a popular psychological theory of the day which claimed that the paranoid person responds to the behavior of others by symbolically organizing a pseudocommunity that is out to get him. His behaviors toward this supposed community produce conflict with the real community around him, who see him as deserving of restraint or retaliation. Lemert's paper is designed to present data showing that the paranoid person reacts differentially to his or her social environment, but that the community around the paranoid is a real one and involves "covertly organized action and conspirational behavior in a very real sense." Lemert is making a customary labeling theoretic move of treating deviance as an act that is interpreted and responded to as deviant by some audience.

> Delusions and associated behavior must be understood in a context of exclusion which attenuates this relationship and disrupts communication. By thus shifting the clinical spotlight away from the individual to a relationship and a process, we make an explicit break with the conception of paranoia as a disease, a state, a condition, or a syndrome of symptoms. Furthermore, we find it unnecessary to postulate trauma of early childhood or arrested psychosexual development to account for the main features of paranoia—although we grant that these and other factors may condition its expression.[59]

For labeling theory, it is the interaction of the person and the environment that produces mental illness, and the accent is upon the environment's (actually, a group's) responses to the person's behavior. In positing this thesis Lemert's tone is almost snide about the psychoanalytic model, but it is clear that his claim about paranoia is not that psychoanalysts are wrong, nor that he is proposing a contradictory hypothesis to theirs, but rather that he has an alternative hypothesis. Thus, he wants to shift attention from the disease notion and to reduce developmental variables from causal to conditioning significance, in order to propose his own positive thesis.

There can be little doubt that in Lemert's work the claims are not primarily, nor do they rest upon, rejections of other models. On the other hand, in the case of some labeling theorists the issue is not so clear. In some of Thomas Scheff's works the basic purpose is to counter other models. For example, among his best known arguments is that physicians err by following the decision rule, "When in doubt, diagnose illness."[60] Scheff contends that psychiatrists make great efforts to avoid taking a Type One error (not treating a sick person), and that as a result of this and other characteristics of psychiatric practice, what mental illness has actually become in the contemporary social world is a social status that one group of persons attaches to another. The persons so labeled come to adopt the role of neurotic, schizophrenic, or whatever they are called, and to exhibit the behaviors expected of that role.

In the full context of Scheff's work, however, one would not want to say that his claims are solely anti-psychiatric, nor that they rest on that foundation. In more recent works in particular,[61] he talks of persons having real psychosocial problems that do not result from labeling, and he considers how they might best be treated. Even the earlier works are not primarily negative theses, but are designed to argue for the labeling explanation of mental illness. In short, the translator would probably not want to place Scheff's version of the labeling model into either of the two camps described above, since there is not clear ground, at least upon this cursory examination, for knowing whether he depends upon opposition to other models in proposing his model.

In the case of another modeler generally classified as a labeling theorist, Thomas Szasz,[62] there is little question that opposition to dominant models is essential to his explanation. Szasz's best known claim is that "mental illness is a myth. Psychiatrists are not concerned with mental illnesses and their treatments. In actual practice they deal with personal, social, and ethical problems in living."[63] He argues in a variety of places, as support for and further development of this position, that diseases must be bodily, and since the mind is not part of the body, it cannot be diseased[64]; that illness implies deviation from norms of functioning for the body whereas mental illness concerns deviations from psychosocial and ethical norms[65]; and that mental health workers, especially psychiatrists, have vested interests in, and thus perpetuate, the myth by treating and studying it. Sometimes he goes quite far in his condemnations:

> It is clear that psychiatrists have a vested interest in diagnosing as mentally ill as many people as possible, just as inquisitors had in branding them as heretics. The 'conscientious' psychiatrist authenticates himself as a competent medical man by holding that sexual deviants (and all kinds of other people, perhaps all of mankind, as Karl Menninger would have it) are mentally ill, just as the 'conscientious' inquisitor authenticated himself as a faithful Christian by holding that homosexuals (and all kinds of other people) were heretics.[66]

Consistently he talks of psychiatrists as persons who enslave or imprison people, and psychiatry as in the service of the state rather than of the client.[67]

Unlike the negative statements about other models or their ontologies found in the authors and models we have discussed thus far, opposition is the *raison d'etre* for the Szaszian model. Without the belligerence toward other models, there is no Szaszian model.[68] This is not because Szasz offers no positive thesis —his hypotheses about mental illness as "problems in living" and his call to understand psychiatric practice and theory by way of their histories and social functions are both positive. The difference from other models is that the Szaszian project appears to be the destruction of other explanations *per se*. Szasz marshalls his positive hypotheses in order to condemn or repudiate other models, not to build an alternative positive explanation of mental illness, a phenomenon which, after all, he says should not be taken to exist, much less to require explanation. A result may be true untranslatability by the essentialist translator (though not necessarily by the extensionalist, as we noted in the previous chapter), at least in those places where what Szasz and his followers want to say about a psychiatric phenomenon is primarily that it does not exist.

In such cases of opposition the translator, true to the motivation for all translation, does not assume untranslatability but rather examines, in usual fashion, the structure of the model. The determination that one essential feature of a model is its antagonism toward what the translator treats as host models does not preempt inquiry into the other essential features. Instead, the essentialist translator may explicate the *grounds* for disagreement, hoping that successful translation might still be possible. His hope stems from the fact that the antagonistic model is critical *about the other model* and thus that there is a common "universe of discourse."

In Szasz's case, there appear to be three grounds for his negative theses about other models: (1) that it is an error to consider suffering persons as patients rather than as some sort of malingerers; (2) that mental illness terms are applied either arbitrarily or ambiguously as a result of not being tied to a physiological notion of illness; and (3) that social control, not medical care, is what one really attends when mental illness is approached by the usual models. Were we offering this analysis for an actual translation, rather than for purposes of illustration, detailed evidence would be presented for concluding that these are the essential grounds. For now suffice it to say that we find these to be the contentions used in various ways in making Szasz's specific claims against the standard models of mental illness.

Given these grounds, it is apparent that any claim sentence from Szaszian theory will come out in standard psychological models at best in self-critical language. With adequate specification, however, the claim might be one that is recognizable as worthy of consideration by the host model. We must keep in mind that the goal of the translator is to re-create the source claim in the host model such that it sounds natural (i.e., not alien) and appreciable to a speaker of the host model-language. In translation of literature this entails retention of the aesthetic qualities of the work within a syntactic, lexical, and stylistic arrangement that a host language audience can be comfortable with. In translation of social science models the parallel needs are retention of the source's declarations with full explanatory power within a way of talking that is appealing to adherents of the host model.

Toward this end the translator might concentrate upon breaking down these essential grounds of the Szaszian model—without being reductionistic or trivializing the model—into the sorts of items which bring them in line with host model concerns, asking questions of Szasz's texts such as the following: Which specific errors are the psychological models making? How can we recognize these as errors? What would count as non-arbitrary or unambiguous usage of terms? How do we know when we have medical care rather than social control? As applied to at least some of his specific claim sentences, these questions appear likely to produce possibilities for translation. For instance, a basic Szaszian claim sentence about schizophrenia comes out: schizophrenia is a mythological disease because it does not result from pathological processes at the anatomical level.[69] Without much work we can see easy routes to translation of this claim into the more biochemical models, but routes to a diagram that permits translation to psychological models are also visible, even though the claim sentence is so unfriendly. Giving full force to his claim by bringing to bear all three of his grounds (rather than only the second), we would seek to specify what counts for Szasz as unambiguously and not arbitrarily a patho-anatomical process, what kind of error is involved in treating "schizophrenics" as "patients," what social control is involved in "schizophrenia," and what would count as medical treatment thereof, and related issues.

In reviewing the relevant texts in which this claim is expounded one finds long diatribes against anti-psychiatrists (who are part of the "soft underbelly of the New Left"[70] and "imprecise, misleading and cheaply self-aggrandizing"[71]), marriage (which is like institutional psychiatry: "neither the matrimonial nor the madness system was created by society to make its members happy or healthy"[72] and "is a trap that often ends in divorce to free those held captive"[73]), and of course psychiatry (which Szasz accuses of "barbarities" and "slavery"[74]). Within these and other discussions appear, however, the arguments for the above claim about schizophrenia.

Specifically, we may unpack the grounds for Szasz's claim as follows: It is an error to consider suffering persons as ill because the correct order in medicine is first to establish morphological pathology and then to name and treat the disease, whereas psychiatry has reversed this for schizophrenia.[75] The basic concept and model of disease on Szasz's view is Virchow's, in which one asks "what cells are out of order and what can be done for them."[76] Schizophrenia is said to be considered a disease for quite different reasons: because medical science is about to show a brain abnormality, and because the persons suffer and are hospitalized and treated.[77] Szasz sums up this part of his argument as follows:

> The point I want to emphasize here is that each of these terms (for schizophrenia) refers to behavior, not disease; to disapproved conduct, not to histopathological change; hence they may loosely be called 'conditions', but they are not, strictly speaking, medical conditions.[78]

Closely related to these issues are his grounds for what would count nonarbitrarily and unambiguously as an illness in regard to schizophrenia. Here Szasz is less clear. On the one hand, he implies that if Kraepelin and Blueler had discovered "histopathological lesions or pathophysiological processes" in their patients, instead of acting as if they had discovered such, they would have uncovered an actual disease.[79] He proposes that if we have a brain disease, we should study the brain, not the patient's thinking, and that we cannot study the anatomical level by showing that schizophrenics respond to various treatments assumed to be operating at the anatomical level.[80] On the other hand, he emphasizes that "schizophrenia is not a disease, but only the name of an alleged disease"[81] and he takes a radically lexical determinist position:

> (I)f there is no psychiatry, there can be no schizophrenics. In other words, the identity of an individual as a schizophrenic depends on the existence of the social system of (institutional) psychiatry. Hence, if psychiatry is abolished, schizophrenics disappear. This does not mean that certain kinds of persons who might

previously have been schizophrenics, or who might like to be schizophrenics, also disappear; there assuredly remain persons who are incompetent, or self-absorbed, or who reject their "real" roles, or who offend others in some other ways. But if there is no psychiatry, none of them can be schizophrenic.... It would, of course, be absurd to seek the advancement of the slave within the slave system, and in particular from his master. It is similarly absurd to seek the "treatment" of the schizophrenic within the psychiatric system....[82]

Presumably, Szasz does not mean to contradict himself here by saying both that schizophrenia could be an illness (if physiological pathology is shown) and that schizophrenia is nothing but a word. Rather, he seems to be pessimistic about the possibility of finding the kind of clear pathology he requires, at least for very many "schizophrenics,[83]" and is characterizing *what* schizophrenia *has been*, from the beginnings of psychiatry through the present. Indeed, Szasz has proposed that is "pathophysiological or neurochemical abnormalities" of schizophrenia are demonstrated, "then schizophrenia, too, will be a disease.[84]"

Of the treatment of "schizophrenics," Szasz contends that psychiatry is a form of control of persons who behave in ways that others do not like, and thus is not medical treatment.[85] A key factor supposed to reveal this state of affairs is that often in psychiatry persons are given treatments they do not want, whereas in "traditional medicine" they seek treatment.[86] The social control element comes out for Szasz also when he looks at the list of symptoms used to diagnose schizophrenia and notes that "the briefest critical scrutiny of this list makes its scientific and medical pretentions vanish." He notes that delusions, inappropriate behavior, hallucinations, and over- or under-activity describe features of almost everyone's behavior—e.g., "that gold will always be worth $35 an ounce," was a popular delusion, invading Vietnam was inappropriate or unusual, and "travelling half-way across the world to attend a psychiatric meeting" is over-activity.[87]

Moreover, the major "treatment" psychiatrists have given to "patients" is confinement, Szasz claims, whereas if they were behaving like proper medical doctors, they would have determined whether the persons were actually (somatically) sick and then treated them accordingly. To treat medically means for Szasz "to cure disease, not to control deviance.[88]" Given what schizophrenia is at present, however, the proper course of treatment is not of the patient, but must take place, non-medically, at the societal level:

In short, madman and mad-doctor, psychotic and psychiatrist, are locked in an embrace of mutual coercion, confusion and confirmation.... There is no problem of schizophrenia for psychiatry to solve. But there is a problem of schizophrenia-cum-psychiatry for epistemology and ethics, for philosophy and law, for society as a group and for individuals as moral agents to confront with the intelligence and to reconcile with their conscience.[89]

With this unpacking in hand, the essentialist translator has her material for constructing diagrams of the claim sentence. The resulting diagram might look like Figure 11. (In an actual translation the diagram would be constructed

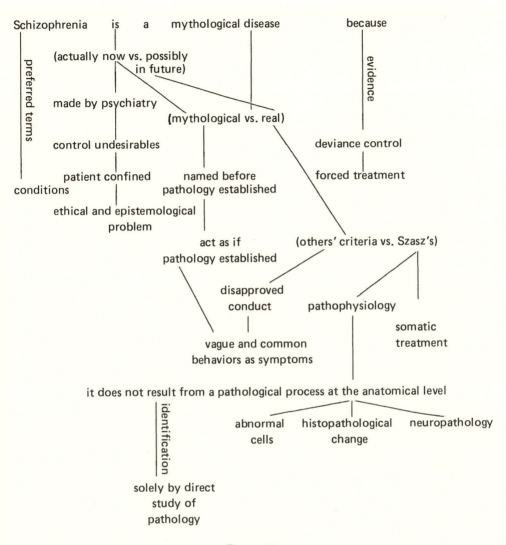

Figure 11

using not merely the material derived from this developmental analysis, but also from the outcomes of analyses of definitions.)

In reading around this diagram, the translator finds, for example, that Szasz divides schizophrenia into two conditions, that which exists now and that which may exist in the future. At present we have a condition that is made by psychiatry, in the control of undesirables, with patients confined to hospitals, and ethical and epistemological problems. All of this entails an entity considered mythological because it was named before pathology was established, with persons acting as if pathology was established, and using vaguely identified and common behaviors as symptoms. The use of these behaviors as symptoms also results from their connection with disapproved conduct, and both the conduct and the behaviors are what other modelers take to be criteria for the disease. Meanwhile, Szasz says that possibly in the future schizophrenia will become a real disease, which means it will be treated somatically and will be identified solely by the direct study of pathophysiology, which means either abnormal cells, histopathological change, or neuropathology.

Step Three: Movement to the Host Model

With a full diagram, the translator is ready to move from the source to the host model, armed with this reading of the claim sentence by way of the essential grounds and ideas of the model as elaborated for the particular claim.

In the host model the translator makes approximately the same moves as above, but the starting and ending points are determined by whether the translator seeks a partial or a complete translation, and by whether the translation is conducted primarily for the sake of the source, the host, or for balanced considerations.

Decisions between partial and complete translations are made on the same sorts of grounds that natural language translators use: Will the host accept only a partial translation? Is a complete translation linguistically unwieldy in the host model? Do untranslatable units appear in the elaborated claim sentence that obviate complete translation? Complete translation is the translator's goal, of course, but not his expectation. Deciding between partial and complete translations depends upon decisions about which model will be emphasized (and vice versa). Most natural language translation is conducted with emphasis on the host language, which is typically the translator's native tongue. In translation of models one must ask whether the translation is primarily to bring the source claim to the host, to initiate dialogue between the models, to show the host that the source has something worthwhile to say, and similar concerns.

To remain, for convenience, with our Szaszian claim, note that a complete translation into any other model is likely to result in long, cumbersome statements, whereas a complete translation might be possible in the long run by translating part-by-part. Substantial differences will result if one opts for bringing testable claims from Szasz to the host, making Szasz's claims clearer to the host, enriching the host by allowing it to include some Szaszian concerns in its own terms, or related possibilities.

The precise moves the translator makes will depend upon those decisions. Suppose we are translating in order to encourage the test of Szaszian claims in a psychological model. This would suggest a partial translation, because the host modelers will want to operationalize the claim and delimit it to something with which they can conduct experiments or other kinds of observations. The translator would then select a partial claim, employing the essentialist criterion that it entail major and fundamental components of the larger claim and that it be complete on its own terms. Thus, the translator might choose from Figure 11, "schizophrenia is currently used by psychiatrists to control persons considered undesirables," for a very partial translation.

Once such a choice is made, the translator then turns to the host model, still keeping in mind the various connections of this fragment within the source diagram, and seeks to identify where in the host such issues arise. This involves reading texts in the psychological host model until one finds materials on schizophrenia, the work of psychiatrists, control of patients, patient desirability, and so forth. When these items are identified, the statements about them are connected to the essential features of the host model, using the same tools as before (definitional and developmental analyses). In the host's case, however, there is no single claim sentence to diagram, and instead the translator diagrams any claims he or she can find that somehow overlap with parts of the source sentence diagram or with the source model's essences. For instance, if we find that a host model talks about when to hospitalize a patient, we associate this with the source diagram's issue of "control of undesirables" and thus would want to ascertain how statements about hospitalization are affiliated with the host's essential grounds for claim making or its essential ideas. In addition, one would want to check anything in the host that concerns ambiguity of diagnosis, since this is related to one of the source's three essential grounds for claim making.

Eventually, the translator will develop a collection of essentialist diagrams of the host, where it overlaps with the source, and from these will derive the ways of talking about the source claim in the host model. Thus, if one of the host's diagrams turns out similar to Figure 12, we can imagine how part of the translated sentence might look in the psychological host model.

The translator might consider, everything else being amenable, a partial translation of Szasz along this sort of format: "Characteristics $A_1 \ldots A_n$ are necessary and sufficient for treating a person as schizophrenic in $B_1 \ldots B_n$ ways." In this translation A = those characteristics of the person that are damaging or undesirable to others in the community, and B = treatments that control the person. From the diagram above we can begin to fill in this sort of translation in host language: "The characteristics of bothering others by being unclean, by carrying diseases, by having nowhere to live, by displaying delusions, by talking in word salads or by $(A_6 \ldots A_n)$ are necessary and sufficient for treating persons as schizophrenic by hospitalizing them or by $(B_2 \ldots B_n)$." Needless to say, this sentence is not straightforward in terms of most psychological models, and might be received with some suspicion. It is, however, in the host model's language, and does set up conditions that can be tested. With it the host can explore, for example, whether bothering others in these ways, in the absence of danger to the patient himself, results in hospitalization, or whether persons are hospitalized even if they do not bother others; i.e., the sufficiency and necessity stipulations may be checked.

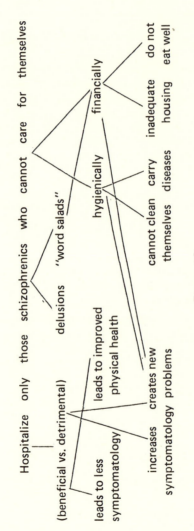

Figure 12

Notes

1. See the "Metaphysics" in W.D. Ross, ed., *The Works of Aristotle* (Oxford: Clarendon Press, 1931), 1022a and 1028a.

2. *Ibid.*, 1029b.

3. *Ibid.*, 1030a.

4. More, *Posterior Analytics* I.22.83a, 25–28.

5. John Locke, *An Essay Concerning Human Understanding* (New York: Meridian, 1964), Book 3, Chapter VI, Section 4.

6. W.V. Quine, *From a Logical Point of View* (Cambridge: Harvard University Press, 1961).

7. *Ibid.*, p. 155. Quine has talked recently of contextual sorts of analyticity, suggesting that he may not be antagonistic to a pragmatic essentialist strategy such as ours.

8. See Karl Popper, *Conjectures and Refutations* (New York: Basic Books, 1962). Popper discusses essentialism as a certain view of scientific theories which for him is comprised of the following two doctrines:

    > The scientist can succeed in finally establishing truth of such theories beyond all reasonable doubt; and the best, the truly scientific theories, describe the "essences" or the "essential natures" of things—the realities which lie behind the appearances (pp. 103–104).

    Popper is especially critical of the latter doctrine, for he regards it as playing an "obscurantist" role in science, or at least in our thought about science. If the doctrine were adopted and if a theory of essences were by some lucky accident hit upon, Popper holds that some very fruitful questions could never be posed, for the path of inquiry would be cut short. Gradually, then, the essentialist doctrine collapses into the former one of ultimate explanation (p. 115). However, it is clear that essentialism need not be limited to a realist doctrine of ultimate and eternal verities, which is the rather limited and extreme interpretation Popper addresses.

9. Edmund Husserl, *Ideas* (New York: Collier, 1962), p. 14.

10. Edmund Husserl, *The Crisis of European Sciences* (Evanston, Illinois: Northwestern University Press, 1970).

11. Husserl, *Ideas*.

12. Eli Hirsch, "Essence and Identity," in Milton Munitz et al., eds., *Identity and Individuation* (New York: New York University Press, 1971).

13. *Ibid.*, p. 33.

14. *Ibid.*, p. 33.

15. *Ibid.*, p. 33.

16. *Ibid.*, p. 34.

17. Daniel Bennett, "Essential Properties," *Journal of Philosophy* 66, (1969): 487–499.

18. *Ibid.*, p. 491.

19. *Ibid.*, p. 498.

20. *Ibid.*, pp. 496–498.

21. *Ibid.*, p. 498.

22. Some selected recent writings on these topics follow.

    Hilary Putnam's writings on necessity bear especially on the tenability of essentialism. See, for example, "It Ain't Necessarily So," in Jay Rosenberg and Charles Travis, eds., *Readings in the Philosophy of Language* (Englewood Cliffs, New Jersey: Prentice-Hall, 1971); and "Is Semantics Possible?" and "Meaning and Reference," in Steven P. Schwartz, ed., *Naming, Necessity and Natural Kinds* (Ithaca: Cornell University Press, 1977). Saul Kripke's work has enlivened interest in essentialism along these lines as well. See "Naming and Necessity," in

Donald A. Davidson and Gilbert Harman, eds., *Semantics of Natural Languages* (Dordrecht: Reidel, 1972).

For a view of essences in terms of possible worlds different from that of Kripke, see Alvin Plantinga, "World and Essence," *Philosophical Review* 79, (1970): 461–492.

For a recent argument for the existence of natural kinds see Douglas Browning, "Believing in Natural Kinds," *The Southwestern Journal of Philosophy* 9, (1978): 135–148.

Articles on essentialism and modal quantification in logic include Ruth Barcan Marcus, "Essentialism in Modal Logic," *Nous* 1, (1967): 91–96; and "Essential Attributes," *Journal of Philosophy* 68, (1971): 187–192. Also Terence Parsons, "Grades of Essentialism and Quantified Modal Logic," *Philosophical Studies* 29, (1976): 181–191; and "Essentialism and Quantified Modal Logic," *Philosophical Review* 78, (1969): 35–52.

23. Barry Glassner, *Essential Interactionism: On the Intelligibility of Prejudice* (London: Routledge and Regan Paul, 1980).

24. Jerome Rabow, Jorja Manos, and Lauir Engleberg, "Separate Realities: A Comparison Study of Estians, Psychoanalysands, and Untreated," *Small Group Behavior* 10, (1979): 445–474.

25. Claude Levi-Strauss, *Structural Anthropology*.

26. *Ibid.*, p. 217.

27. There are debates within the structuralist movement about whether structures are essential. This arises apparently in part from the posing by advocates of both positions, of phenomenology and structuralism as opposites. We will call structures "fundamental to" or "generative of" models, rather than "essential to."

28. Philip Pettit, *The Concept of Structuralism* (Berkeley: University California Press, 1975), p. 87.

29. Terence S. Turner, "Oedipus: Time and Structure in Narrative Form," in Robert Spencer, ed., *Forms of Symbolic Action* (Seattle: American Ethnological Society, 1969), p. 30.

30. Octavio Paz, *Claude Levi-Strauss* (New York: Dell, 1970), p. 37.

31. Sigmund Freud, *The Complete Psychological Works* (London: Hogarth Press, 1966), Vol. 19, pp. 256 and 289–297.

32. Sigmund Freud, *A General Introduction to Psychoanalysis* (New York: Simon and Schuster, 1963), pp. 289–297.

33. To the extent that there is binary opposition, in Freud's work it is between incest-wish and incest-anxiety (the Oedipus and Castration complexes) (L. Frey-Rohen, *From Freud to Jung*, New York: Putnam, 1974, p. 145), or is the claim that Oedipus Complex "is twofold, positive and negative... due to the bisexuality originally present in children... A boy has not merely an ambivalent attitude towards his father and an affect object-choice towards his mother, but at the same time he also behaves like a girl and displays... a feminine attitude to his father ... ." (Freud, *The Ego and The Id*, New York: Norton, 1960, p. 23).

34. Sherry Turkel, *Psychoanalytic Politics* (New York: Basic Books, 1978).

35. Turner, "Oedipus," pp. 42, 58, and 75–76.

36. In light of Noam Chomsky's works some readers may wonder that we have ignored what might be taken as a theory of those structures that generate language and perhaps claims. Although we would be pleased to entertain an argument for this sort of translation strategy, we doubt that it would be essentialist, because in Chomsky's work not even deep structures are taken to be essential, since other structures could have produced the same surface structures. In any event, we are unable to locate in the literature a strategy for translation built upon Chomsky's work. The closest efforts at such have been criticized by Nida ("A Framework for the Analysis and Evolution of Theories of Translation," in *Translation: Applications and Research*, edited by Richard Brislin, New York: Gardner, 1976, pp. 69–75), on the grounds that meaning is defined in terms of propositional equivalence, that an ideal speaker and hearer are assumed, and that contexts of speech are omitted.

37. George Santayana, *The Realm of Essence* (New York: Scribners, 1927), p. 23.

38. Rudner, *Philosophy of Social Sciences.*

39. Robert Wolfson, in remarks at a memorial symposium for Richard Rudner, Washington University, St. Louis, 1980; to be published in *Synthese.*

40. Max Scheler, *Problems of a Sociology of Knowledge* (London: Routledge and Kegan Paul, 1980), p. 34.

41. John Hospers, *An Introduction to Philosophical Analysis* (Routledge and Kegan Paul, 1956), p. 39.

42. In some cases, however, modelers use "operational definitions," which cut between Aristotle's two types, since they are said to be observable indicators of real properties of the thing (cf., P.W. Bridgman, *The Logic of Modern Physics*, New York: Macmillan, 1954).

43. Some linguistic philosophers argue that definitions suggest not essences but only how we use the language. Glassner (*Essential Interactionism*) has offered evidence that identifying features of phenomena may be uncovered through analyses of definitions. For our present purposes, however, we require no more than that definitions help the translator to specify the characteristic ways in which modelers use their talk about the claims being translated.

44. Robert Bolton, "Essentialism and Semantic Theory in Aristotle," *The Philosophical Review* 85, (1976): pp. 514–544.

45. Leland Hinsie and Robert Campbell, *Psychiatric Dictionary* (London: Oxford University Press, 1960), p. 188.

46. Sigmund Freud, *Beyond the Pleasure Principle*, Complete Works, Vol. 18.

47. Webster's New World Dictionary, 1962, p. 658 and so forth.

48. This is developed from statements throughout Durkheim's *Suicide* (New York: Free Press, 1966), and most directly stated on pp. 297–300.

49. Durkheim, *Suicide*, p. 46.

50. *Ibid.*, p. 310.

51. *Ibid.*, pp. 309–10.

52. *Ibid.*, p. 181.

53. Freud, *Complete Works*, Vol. 3, p. 279. We wish to thank Stipe Mestrovic for ideas and references in this paragraph.

54. For example, Thomas Scheff, *Being Mentally Ill* (Chicago: Aldine, 1966): Roger Bastide, *The Sociology of Mental Disorder* (New York: David McKay, 1972); and Thomas Szasz, *The Myth of Mental Illness* (New York, Harper, 1961).

55. Sigmund Freud, *Civilization and Its Discontents* (London: Hogarth Press, 1959), p. 142. See also *The Complete Works*, Vol. 19, p. 205.

56. Freud, *Complete Works*, Vol. 20, postscript, p. 72.

57. Bastide, *Sociology of Mental Disorders*, pp. 22 and 105.

58. Edwin Lemert, "Paranoia and the Dynamics of Exclusion," *Sociometry*, 25 (1962), pp. 2–20.

59. *Ibid.*, p. 4.

60. Scheff, *Being Mentally Ill*, pp. 110–11.

61. Thomas Scheff, forthcoming from University of California Press.

62. Szasz (in personal communication) denies this affiliation, apparently based on his emphasis on the moral dimensions of treatment, his nonacceptance of labeling as a causal explanation for "mental illnesses," and his desire to call for individuals' responsibility, rather than society's, for mental well being.

63. Thomas Szasz, *Law, Liberty, and Psychiatry* (New York: Macmillan, 1963), p. 296.

64. Szasz, *Myth*, p. 11; and *Second Sin* (Garden City: Anchor, 1974), p. 109.

65. Thomas Szasz, *Ideology and Insanity* (Garden City: Anchor, 1970), p. 15; and *Myth*, p. 41.

66. Thomas Szasz, *The Manufacture of Madness* (New York: Harper and Row, 1970), p. 175.

67. Szasz, *Law*.

68. It could be argued that there is another side to Szasz that makes his model more readily available. In various places, most notably in *Pain and Pleasure* (New York: Basic, 1957), Szasz is a faithful psychoanalyst, as he is in much of his teaching. The translator could treat his Freudianism as the hidden grounds for his other statements. To do so, however, would be to erase what is received as the Szaszian model and to ignore that most of his statements in print are opposed to the conventional models.

69. Thomas Szasz, *Schizophrenia* (New York: Basic, 1976); "Correspondence", *British Journal of Psychiatry*, 130, (1977): 520–521; and "Schizophrenia: The Sacred Symbol of Psychiatry," *British Journal of Psychiatry*, 129, (1976): 308–316.

70. Szasz, *Schizophrenia*, p. 54.

71. *Ibid.*, p. 48.

72. *Ibid.*, p. 161.

73. *Ibid.*, p. 167.

74. *Ibid.*, pp. 25–26 and 136.

75. Szasz, "Schizophrenia," p. 315.

76. *Ibid.*, p. 310.

77. Szasz, *Schizophrenia*, p. 121.

78. Szasz, "Schizophrenia," p. 311.

79. *Ibid.*, p. 310.

80. *Ibid.*, p. 315 and 312.

81. *Ibid.*, p. 316.

82. Szasz, *Schizophrenia*, pp. 136–37.

83. Szasz, "Schizophrenia," p. 314.

84. Szasz, "Correspondence."

85. Szasz, *Schizophrenia*, p. 108; and "Schizophrenia," p. 314.

86. Szasz, *Schizophrenia*, p. 124.

87. Szasz, "Schizophrenia," p. 313.

88. *Ibid.*, p. 316.

89. Szasz, *Schizophrenia*, p. 197.

6

Examples of Translation Between Models

As a preliminary illustration of the translation strategies, in this concluding chapter we present the results of translations of a claim sentence about depression, from the life events model into Freud's model. In the hope that the translation will be of interest to more than one discipline, and to provide a case where two levels of determinism are considered, we have selected an important sociological model as well as a leading psychological model.

The prominence of the life events model in recent years is evidenced by papers from this perspective in most issues of leading psychiatry journals and its near dominance in specialized forums such as *Journal of Health and Social Behavior*. The stature of Freud's model surely needs no reiteration though some may wonder that we have chosen a model that many consider *passe* and most would contend has been improved and changed throughout this century. While we might have illustrated instead with psychoanalytic theory, which is anyway better clarified in many ways than is Freud himself, one of our goals is to recapture the great works on mental illness. We concur with those who bemoan the losses or "mistranslations" in contemporary social science of the thoughts and findings of the classical thinkers in these fields.

To those familiar with Freud's and life events models, our choice may seem, however, suspiciously fortuitous. "Loss of object" would seem to be at the root of the explanation from each model. For Freud, this explanation is found *per se*, and the events that life events modelers point out as precipitating or causing depression tend to be losses of close relationships. Thus, we could be accused of having selected models with a good deal in common regarding the claim we wish to translate.

The similarity is largely illusory, and this in ways instructive for translations of all sorts. It would be an easy pseudo-translation to consider what the life events modelers see as stressors as simply what Freud called object loss. But in fact the life events modelers are talking in terms of social relations, situational determinism, losses other than those that fit Freud's criteria for object loss, among other differences. Even in the one place we could find where the losses were put by interdisciplinary life events modelers in object loss vocabulary, the interpretation was far from Freud's and remained truly sociological:

> The findings that the exit of an individual from the immediate social field of the respondent is associated more strongly with impairment than comparable entrance emphasizes the importance of object loss in psychopathology in our culture, and suggests that there is a hierarchy of role transformations with respect to psychiatric symptomatology. American society with its secular nontraditional attitudes has left the individual somewhat alone to cope with loss.[1]

Life events modelers do not "see" objects when they talk about the stressors involved in onset of depression, and Freud does not "see" stressors when he talks of object relations. An incommensurabilist could in this context claim that we are misled by the apparent intimacy of the two models, and that these seemingly close translations are just as indeterminate as any others.

There are simpler differences between the models as well, which bring into the translation a further complication. The life events model operates with mainstream contemporary social scientific epistemology; its major findings are statistical correlations between variables. In contrast, Freud's model depends upon case study and development of an organic system of explanation. Another key difference results from the life events model drawing upon a variety of theories (e.g., behaviorist, structural-functional) without having a clear master theory of its own in the way that Freud does. "Although conceptual and theoretical orientations should play an important preparatory role in the design and execution of empirical studies," Judith Rabkin and Elmer Struening suggest, "this does not often appear to be the case in the literature reviewed on the relation of life events, stress and illness.... . The conceptual model is comprehensive, multicausal, and interactive... ."[2] Interestingly, despite this complexity and borrowing from theories, the life events modelers seldom use Freudian thought.

The Claim Sentence

In order to select a claim for this first experiment with the translation strategies, we utilized the standard social scientific and medical indexes, as well as card catalogues, to locate life events model papers and books concerning depression, and on the model more generally. This search produced several dozen papers and books.[3] The topic of depression was chosen because it is a major interest of varieties of both psychiatric and sociological modelers and has been a research concern of the present authors.

One finds, not unexpectedly, a variety of claims about depression from the life events modelers. Many are simply correlational findings, that depressives report many stressful life events prior to the onset of depression, or earlier in life. The various works are distinguished along three dimensions: whether they concern predisposing[4] (relatively early in life) versus precipitating[5] (just before onset of symptoms) events; whether they take stress *per se* as a determining factor or try to ascertain which sorts of events are involved in depression[6]; and whether life events are viewed as causal in their own right or only in conjunction with a separate predisposition (e.g., genetic or developmental[7]). From these pairs of distinctions we have attempted to construct a claim sentence as seemingly distant from Freud's view as possible, in order to make the illustrative translation more challenging and instructive. Thus, we choose a claim concerning specific events taken as precipitating in the strong (direct and causal) sense.

Based upon those sorts of claims and most directly in the work of E.S. Paykel and his associates,[8] we have constructed the following claim sentence:

Exit events play a determining part in clinical depression.

The wording is from the life events modelers and reflects both their strong position and the caution with which they customarily convey that position. "Determining part" suggests direct causation—exit events themselves bring depression—but not a unicausal model of depression, nor any implication that events are final causes. The specificity of type of event is the class labeled "exit," which will be explicated in our diagrams by listing the particular types of events that the modelers classify under this label.

I. An Essentialist Translation

Diagramming the Claim Sentence

In order to develop a diagram of the claim sentence in the source model, we conduct careful readings of texts by source modelers regarding the claim. The definitional and developmental analyses afforded by the life events model are rather limited, however, since the model *per se* has been discussed for only a few decades and has nowhere been systematized in terms of divisions historically or contemporarily, and certainly no dictionary has been produced (as, for example, have several for psychoanalytic models). Nevertheless, we are able through these techniques to explicate the model as applied to this claim sentence. Let us summarize the results of those inquiries, which are displayed in Figure 13.

The first word, *exit*, we determined to have developed within the model during the 1970's, as a result of life events researchers and theorists attempting to specify more clearly the types of events that prove stressful. Most of the early work in life events research set out to demonstrate that life events are correlated with illnesses. Gradually this gave way to attempts for further specificity; the turning point in this development is usually given as 1967,

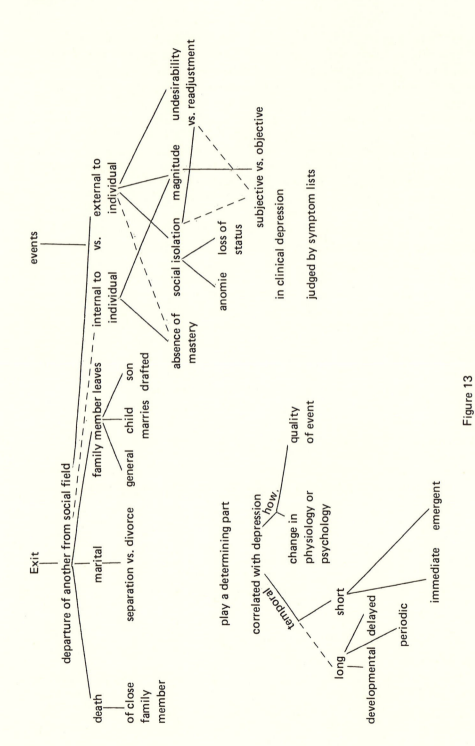

Figure 13

when Holmes and Rahe[9] developed their "Social Readjustment Rating Scale."
This scale was developed by taking many possibly stressful items and asking a
sample of judges to score them for their relative degrees of required readjustment. On the final scale, scores are attached to the 43 items, such as 100 for
death of a spouse, and 12 for vacation. In subsequent research, this scale or
variations upon it have been frequently employed, and many of the items
found in our diagram result from discussions about the scale and the research
involving it. (For instance, below we will discuss "undesirability versus readjustment" from the diagram of *events*, and this debate arose from considerations of whether the major emphasis of Holmes and Rahe on readjustment was
appropriate.)

In the case of depression, a variety of divisions and subdivisions have been
carried out among events lists, using statistical procedures, to see which events
are uniquely correlated with onset of depression. In 1970 Eugene Paykel and
his colleagues[10] proposed that the group of events that together correlate with
depression are what could be considered exit events or "the departure of
another from the individual's social field." They and others had considered
several other possibilities, such as desirable-undesirable, loss of control, sphere
of activity (work, educational, relocation, dating, etc.), and loss more generally
(of jobs, home, etc.). The researchers concluded that the strong and consistent
correlation appeared on the following set of events: death of a close family
member, separation or divorce, or a family member leaving home (including
child marrying or son drafted), and these they called *exit events*. Needless to
say, as with most any model of madness and its substantive explanations, this
is not the only position that life events modelers hold. Some hold that it is
threatening events that give rise to depression, and that only losses over the life
span prove consequential.[11] Others would list many additional sorts of events
as clearly correlated with depression,[12] although there is some strong negative
evidence in this regard, showing that certain types of losses (e.g. of a sibling)
do not result in severe depressions.[13]

Our diagram thus reflects the essential composition of a single position
among life events modelers, albeit a popular one. *Exit* is diagrammed in terms
of the grounds and specification of the claims à la Paykel et al. with the
specific events they so classify. *Events* is diagrammed using a wider essentialist
base, however, since the claim sentence in its utilization of this term depends
upon distinctions among these various core concepts of the model. Whereas
exit was found to be one of several explanatory apexes within the history of the
life events model, *events* is employed throughout the terrain. Thus, we conduct
a kind of definitional analysis of this term, to find its connections to the
foundational concepts of the model.

The following expressions appear often in discussions of the nature of
stressful life events: change (or life changes), readjustment, adaptation (or
coping), magnitude (or severity), noxious stimulus, mastery (or abilities of the
individual), isolation, supports, and desirability and undesirability. In defining

the notions of stressful life events, these are the concepts referred to. When we consider these for inclusion in the class of foundational components in the diagram, some may not be admitted. "Change" is not defining, since all events bring changes, and in our particular instance, exits are necessarily changes. "Adaption" and "supports" are excluded because they are said to be either by-products of the events or missing or unsuccessful elements of responses to the events, rather than defining of the events themselves.[14] "Noxious stimulus," while raised often among the more behaviorist life events modelers, is too theory-dependent for inclusion in a diagram of a claim from that branch of the model that is perhaps most distant from that theory (the claim results from the more sociological end of the model).

To diagram the remaining words, we identified distinctions and oppositions made within the model. A primary distinction made explicitly or implicitly throughout the texts is between those events that arise from the individual and those that arise from outside. The absence of mastery,[15] or inabilities of the individual in relationships or in specific skills, is probably the most frequently cited internal source for events, those often cited are the loss of marital relationships or of children owing to inabilities of the individual who then suffers the loss. Also included is "magnitude," because the modelers point out that events are stressful often as the result of how they are interpreted by the persons suffering them.[16] Another major distinction that one finds upon careful reading is the opposing of undesirability and readjustment. Although these are not obvious contraries, as the model has emerged, the two have become counterposed.[17] We hesitated to include these terms, since the analysis (above) of *exit* suggests that in this particular claim neither undesirability nor readjustment are assumed to be the reason that the events are stressful, but rather they are said to be stressful because the person exits from the social field. But this would be tautological, and thus we must call into play the more general coinage. As it turns out, in the diagram this is not terribly difficult to work out. An additional item, "social isolation,"[18] which usually involves anomie or loss of status, is the missing link. When the modelers say that it is the exit quality of the events *per se* that makes them stressful, they are bringing forward their social assumptions; exits from *social fields* is the topic, and what is said to be stressful is the undesirability or readjustment of the social isolation that exits entail. Thus, the standard reading of the diagram on this point is, "(Exit) events may arise externally to the individual, through the undesirability or readjustment involved in the social isolation they entail." There are other readings, indicated by the broken lines, less often presented but not excluded: "(Exit) events may arise either internally, through either the subjective view of them as socially isolating, as undesirable or involving readjustment, or both"; or, "(Exit) events may arise externally, through their undesirability or readjustment giving rise through subjective interpretations to social isolation, or *vice versa*."

Between the first two words is placed a high level connection, with departure from the social field considered by the modelers primarily as an external event, and thus a solid line is drawn; but with the possibility for considering some cases as internal, and thus a broken line is included in that direction.

Most of the work in essentialist analysis of the phrase, *play a determining part*, occurred during construction of the claim sentence, and is discussed above. At that point a decision was taken to select one of a variety of sorts of causal statements employed by life events modelers. All of that variety, however, depend upon correlational reasoning: The modelers ascertain, and talk of, determinism of life events by way of correlations between the events and the illnesses (or symptoms).[19] Throughout its short development the life events model has adopted this prevailing form of inquiry of contemporary social sciences, and this has become a major, foundational component of the model, since much of what is said within the model depends directly upon this correlational way of looking. In that regard the life events model is akin to some other models and distant from still others. For instance, biochemical models depend upon laboratory experimentation and the talk thereof, whereas the psychoanalytic models utilize case histories and forms of textual analysis, rather than one overriding tool.

There are a couple of matters to unpack with regard to this correlational determinism, since these are areas in which proponents of the model differ. First, on the question of time, some researchers and theorists talk of the determinism as long in duration: That between the time of the stressful event and the onset of illness there is a development period, during which the effects of the event emerge. During this period the event is interpreted, the personality changes, or the social conditions are modified. Others who talk of relatively lengthy periods between events and onset refer to particular illnesses in which this is the case, specifically where there are periodic onsets, as in some affective disorders. Still others suggest that there is simply a delay in the response of the individual to the stressful event. None of these long temporal versions apply, however, to that version of the model from which our claim sentence was developed, and hence in the diagram the line to "long" is broken. Rather, the temporal unit suggested in the major papers[20] concerning this claim is short: The response is implied to be rapid or immediate, or else emergent, by which is meant that symptoms develop gradually from the time of the event to the stage of full blown depression some weeks or months later. Unlike the "long-developmental" version, this does not suggest that something else changes, such as personality or the social environment, since it is assumed that the event itself changes these insofar as they are changed.

In the diagram, only one line, and that a broken line, is drawn from the temporal elements to the *exit* elements. This is simply the least cluttered way we could imagine to indicate that many of the events listed (death of family member, divorce, etc.) could operate with either of the temporal units equally well in any combination, but that marital separation is more likely than the others to involve a long time period.

The other issue brought up in the texts concerning the nature of events determining depression is how this comes about. Frequently life events modelers talk of the events as changing the person's physiology or psychology, either by bringing about a new physiological or psychological state, or by exacerbation or precipitating a long developing condition or predisposition. We include a broken line to this sort of claim, even though those who propound our claim sentence have accepted this possibility, because they *base* their claims not on physiological or psychological changes but upon what they call "the quality of the event."[21] Their position seems to be that it is in the nature of the events themselves that illness is produced; that although not everyone is equally susceptible to the symptom-productive influences of these life events, one need not suffer a structural physiological or psychological change nor exhibit any particular sort of physiological or psychological state prior to the event in order to be affected.

The brief and simple part of the diagram for *in clinical depression* surprised us as much as it may some readers. In careful examination of the life events model texts regarding our claim sentence, we found that all ascertained whether persons were clinically depressed on the basis of applications of symptom lists. These lists vary in their complexity and details, and in some cases the researchers simply used patients diagnosed by hospital staffs, who use primarily symptom lists, to compose their samples. In one way, this apparent simplicity is quite damaging to our translation, since we cannot compare definitions of depression, or parts of these definitions, with those discussed at some length in Freud's work.

Before turning to Freud's model, we can, however, compare the two models' views of this phenomenon of depression, as distinguished from other phenomena. A basic distinction is between serious depression and ordinary or less severe conditions. For Freud, the distinction is between mourning and melancholia, for the life events modelers between common grief and sadness/depression. Life events modelers appear to accept that there is a distinction,[22] and Freud makes a major point of the difference in his "Mourning and Melancholia." We have adapted some diagrammatic techniques mentioned in Chapter 2 in order to prepare a graphic description of the distinctions in the two models (Figure 14).

Freud suggests several differences between mourning and melancholia, the most recognizable being our ability to explain mourning as a conscious and ordinary process that the ego undergoes after a loss.[23] Following Abraham, Freud considered both mourning and melancholia to be responses to losses, with melancholia the consequence of an unconsciously experienced loss, and mourning a reaction to a known loss. As we shall see below, in Freud's view the physical processes are key differentia between the two, with incorporation of the lost object the core process in melancholia but not in mourning.

Indicators		Problem
Freud	**Life Events**	
explained by conscious process		
known loss		Mourning
	mild symptoms	Common sadness
	no major stressors	
Object incorporated into ego		- - - - - melancholia - - - - - -
loss of loved one		
unconscious	real world loss	
loss of capacity to love		
ego emptied		
characteristic	usual symptoms	- - - - - depression - - - - - -
mental features	uniquely modern	

Figure 14

Both models list the loss of loved one—taken broadly to include even roles and values by Freud[24]—as characteristically present in melancholia. They depart where Freud talks of unconscious loss and of the loss of ability to love, whereas for life events modelers the person suffers a real world loss (and loss of anyone *to* love). Both modelers, in their unique vocabularies, talk of identifying melancholia or depression by the behaviors exhibited. Freud lists pretty much the same behaviors (loss of interests, sadness, etc.) and calls them "characteristic mental features,"[25] whereas life events modelers talk of symptoms and tend to use the lists devised for clinical or research purposes.[26] Life events modelers also depart from Freud by considering depressive reactions a uniquely modern problem that occurs in response to intense stress from loss events, because moderns are "left alone to cope (and) grief and mourning are denied to a larger extent in our society than in many others."[27]

Diagrams of the Host
As suggested in Chapter 5, diagrams of the host model cannot be reduced to a specific and well defined claim, since one would not know which such claim to choose. The diagrams are instead of those lexical units in the host which the bilingual translator identifies as concerning phenomena or issues similar to those found in the source diagram. Again the diagram is constructed by way of

definitional and developmental analyses of how these items are built upon the essential components of the model.

Of the first words of the source diagram, there appears a seemingly close similarity early in Freud's famous essay, "Mourning and Melancholia," when he suggests that melancholia is in some persons produced by the loss of a loved one or of "some abstraction which has taken the place of one, such as one's country, liberty, an ideal, and so on."[28] He specifically notes that the loss may be by way of death of the loved one, or by other means such as being jilted, slighted, neglected or disappointed.[29] In a later essay he appears quite close to the life events way of talking: "It is no unusual thing for a man to acquire a melancholic depression and an inhibition in his work as a result of his father's death."[30] Immediately, however, Freud builds these contentions upon his own model and thereby departs from the life events modeler. On the same page just quoted, for instance, he continues: "His mourning over the loss of his father is the more likely to turn to melancholia, the more his attitude to him bore the stamp of ambivalence." He also suggests that the melancholia is not an end, but rather an indicator of deeper changes in the person's very nature.

In establishing the distinction between mourning and melancholia, he suggests that the losses involved in both cases are *object* losses, and that melancholia is distinguished from mourning by only the former involving a loss that is *unconscious*.[31]

That these terms are fundamental components of Freud's model would be difficult to question. *Object* is employed often by Freud in building his explanations of instinct, sexuality, development, love, and other topics, and he combines the term to form other key concepts in his model, such as object choice, object love, object cathexis, object relationship, and object loss. The "discovery" of the *unconscious* is often considered among the most important of Freud's achievements. It is difficult to imagine most of Freud's analyses without this concept, since his psychoanalytic method emphasizes that psychic life and psychopathology derive from the unconscious,[32] and the analyst is called upon to bring persons to uncover the contents of their unconscious.

Let us consider, then, Freud's version of the loss involved in depression, as diagrammed in Figure 15. For him, there is an object loss (i.e., a person or substitute to which the subject related himself is removed) and this is suffered unconsciously (i.e., the subject is unaware of what about the loss is of significance for him).[33] The operative unconscious process consists in a kind of transformation, which turns the object loss into an ego-loss. Freud explains that in depression the libido is not withdrawn from the lost object and displaced on a new object, but instead is displaced onto the ego, and there is an identification of the ego with the abandoned object. The lost object is taken in, narcissistically, as if it were the ego.[34] The object is then tormented for having abandoned the subject or for something that has long bothered the subject, but this torment is now internal to the subject and produces the characteristic symptoms of depression.[35] Freud concludes that there are three

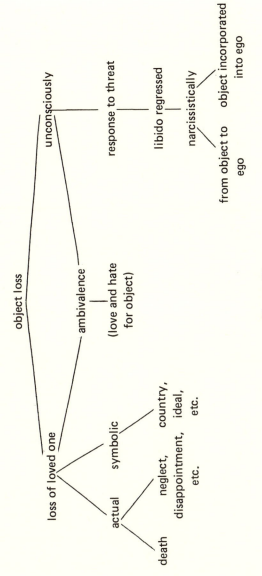

Figure 15

preconditions of depression—"loss of object, ambivalence, and regression of libido into the ego."[36]

It turns out, upon both developmental and definitional analyses, that in explicating the basic claim about object loss and the unconscious Freud employs several additional basic units: narcissism, ego, ambivalence, regression, and libido. We see this from the above description of his way of building the explanation of the connection between object loss and melancholia, and also by noting that these seven terms are the only ones[37] used regularly by Freud in his discussions of the others, and these are widely recognized as key fundamental concepts of his model. Connections among these concepts emerge in reading through the texts in which the concepts appear in discussions of depression, or in considerations of other topics where they are used in similar ways to their applications *re* depression. That the seven concepts are the building blocks is evidenced by the fact that in those passages Freud relies upon the others when discussing any single concept from the list, or else resorts to everyday notions to explain or define these.

The results of this reading appear as Figure 15. At the left is material already discussed, regarding the everyday language version of what Freud says is lost in the type of object loss involved in depression. This loss of a loved one is said to be an ambivalent emotion, however, by which Freud appears to mean that both love and hate for the object are present.[38] This ambivalence is at the unconscious level and productive of the self-reproach after the loss.[39] More importantly for Freud, however, is another unconscious process occurring in depression; regression of libido into the ego is said to distinguish the etiology of depression from that of other psychic problems.[40] Here we find Freud using libido in a manner in which he customarily used the concept in his less sexually oriented theorizing, as mental energy. In what have come to be called "the Fliess papers," Freud wrote 20 year before "Mourning and Melancholia" that "it would not be far wrong... to start from the idea that melancholia consists in mourning over loss of libido"[41] and proposed a schematic physiological explanation involving sexual anesthesia. As noted in Chapter 5, by the time of "Mourning and Melancholia" Freud has moved far into the psychological and partly sociological theorizing that characterizes his lasting contributions. In that paper the libido is no longer said to be lost. Rather, he wants to say that this energy is narcissistically transmitted, thus carrying forth his work on narcissism in the usual way: in terms of the economy between ego-libido and object-libido. Normally a person is said to be sending out libido to objects and receiving libido back from those objects, whereas in depression (among other conditions) the relationships outward toward the object disappear and libido is continually pent up.[42] It is said to be a kind of attention to the self that derives from having identified with the lost object, "the result of which is that in spite of the conflict with the loved person, the love-relation need not be given up."[43] The narcissistic libido serves as a response to the threat entailed in the loss of object.[44]

Developmental analysis proves important also in examination of *regression*, a notion Freud introduced in 1900 in "The Interpretation of Dreams" as a kind of movement backward, of images arising from various psychical systems, until the dream returns to rather primitive systems. Just after that time, in his analysis of the case of Dora, Freud proposed the basic psychic process he would use to explain melancholia, but in this earlier period sexuality was a key essence of his model, whereas in the later work on melancholia, ego relations replaced most of the sexual orientation. "It is impossible," Freud wrote in the early work, "to avoid the suspicion that, when the ideas attaching to certain excitations are incapable of becoming conscious, those excitations must act upon one another differently, run a different course, and manifest themselves differently from those other excitations which we describe as 'normal' and which have ideas attaching to them of which we become conscious."[45]

It was not until 1914, however, that Freud returned to the issue in order to develop the notion in the way it is used in 1915 in "Mourning and Melancholia." He added a passage to the earlier "Interpretation of Dreams" in 1914, which added to the topographical regression he had been considering in that paper, two other forms of regression: formal (a return to primitive methods of expression) and temporal (where a problem brings back earlier psychical structures).[46] Regressions regarding objects—the concern in Freud's analysis of depression—are of the temporal order.[47]

Freud talks of the depressive's regression as a movement away from the object and back to "original narcissism," by which he means the process found in early (oral stage) development, wherein the ego tries to make the object part of itself.[48] The basic argument is that "so immense is the ego's self-love... and so vast is the amount of narcissistic libido which we see liberated in the fear that emerges at a threat to life" that the ego will not "consent to its own destruction,"[49] and so "by taking flight into the ego love escapes extinction."[50] This flight is made possible by regression, but at the conscious level all that is felt is a severe conflict within the ego, in the form of self-criticism and worthlessness.[51]

In terms of our own developmental analysis, the conflict described here is an early hint of what Freud would develop in the decade after "Mourning and Melancholia" as *superego*.[52] In "Mourning and Melancholia" he refers to "the critical agency" as that part of the ego structure involved in the conflict, but *ego* is used in the relatively undifferentiated manner characteristic of Freud's work prior to his "second theory" (where, beginning principally in 1920, ego becomes a system). The ego is treated during the writings about melancholia as the unconscious self, but always the self functioning in specific ways. Freud is extending his earlier thesis that "no experience could have a pathogenic effect unless it appeared intolerable to the subject's ego and gave rise to efforts at defense."[53] In earlier writings the ego functions (in summary and chronologically) to inhibit or as an agency of defense, as a carrier of wishes, as a tester of reality, in conflict with sexual instincts, as a sexual object, and as a reservoir of libido. In "Mourning" the ego functions in complex ways that utilize and extend this progression in Freud's usage: The libido set free from the object-relationship (cathexis) locates within the ego[54]; the ego is active in its involvement with objects[55]; and the ego is a place itself that also has its own subregions.[56] Later, in "The Ego and the Id," this last point is further specified, when Freud says that melancholia involves the superego and is based on a conflict between the ego and superego. Over the course of Freud's work on melancholia, the ego becomes that functioning unconscious selfhood where narcissistically regressed libido locates in the face of ambivalence, and where the ambivalence is played out.

Figure 15 will be utilized as a reminder of what was summarized in the preceding discussion, in order to help identify possible areas of overlap between the source and host applications of their respective essential units to the topics at hand. First, however, we need to perform similar analyses of units from Freud that relate to the other words within the source diagram, and display these findings diagrammatically.

On the issue of determinism Freud's position is notoriously difficult to specify, since he nowhere specifies it clearly. He usually holds to a temporality that might be called the present past,[57] in which problems in the adult are extensions of childhood neurosis that was not overcome: "Every neurosis in an adult is built upon a neurosis which has occurred in his childhood but has not invariably been severe enough to strike the eye and be recognized as such."[58] Whether melancholia is for Freud just another neurosis is unclear, however, because he never calls melancholia a neurosis, and we have already seen that he does not discuss childhood antecedents when considering the nature of melancholia, but rather talks of immediate losses. Nevertheless, it would appear that the presence of the past in the case of melancholia is the ambivalence about the lost object.

Freud does hold to a hard determinist position. He repeatedly makes the point expressed most strongly in the sixth of his introductory lectures on psychoanalysis, that we "nourish a deeply rooted faith in undetermined psychical events and in free will, but that this is quite unscientific and must yield to the demand of a determinism whose rule extends over mental life."[59] What is in doubt is the form of that determinism. In several places he seems to favor the notion that psychical life is *motivated* and that there are typically a complex of motive-determinants for any psychic phenomenon.[60] As we have already described, in melancholia several processes within the person are said to be involved, and this is consistent with views he espoused much earlier, for example, "A single symptom corresponds to several meanings simultaneously."[61]

In other places Freud sounds like a regular causalist, as when he talks of "the existence of a causal connection between Leonardo's relation with his mother in childhood and his later manifest, if ideal (sublimated), homosexuality."[62] Sometimes the causation is also immediate: "Unconscious ideas—or better, the unconsciousness of certain mental processes—are the direct cause of the morbid symptoms."[63] And yet he emphasizes *processes* more often than causes and is fond of terms like *realize, express,* and *announce* where others might talk in terms of cause. Overall, we are most comfortable describing Freud's version of the determinism of melancholia with this summary (as in Figure 16): The current psychical processes (as described above) motivate the melancholic symptoms and are built upon the ground[64] of ambivalence that has been developing since childhood.

Developing the Host Sentence

We now seek overlaps between the source and host derivations from their respective essential bases, to the issues at hand. We will propose five translated sentences of the source claim, each attempting to fulfill different ambitions of the translator regarding balance of the models and use to which the translation will be put. Our technique is to compare the various diagrams that resulted from our essentialist analyses of the source and host with regard to issues raised by the claim sentence. We use those parallel parts of the diagrams, sticking as closely as possible to host wording but supplementing where necessary with everyday language expressions. In discussing these proposed translation sentences we will not reiterate the above analysis of the two models but rather will simply use the conclusions reached there. For reasons suggested in Chapter 2, the translator of material that is not solely technical and fully systematized by way of formal logic can explain and define his or her efforts but cannot provide within reasonable space limitations an explication of each decision taken in the process of translating.

Our proposed translations are as follows:

1. *General, model-balanced*: "The loss of a family member may be an object loss that threatens the ego and motivates melancholia."

This first translation is short and simple and tries to balance the two models. The types of loss noted in the life events claim are summarized as "loss of a family member," thereby sacrificing source model specificity, most especially in the total neglect of the nature of "events" as seen in that model (e.g., that the quality of the event as undesirable or socially isolating is crucial and of the source's correlational causalism). Neglect is directed at the host model, and at

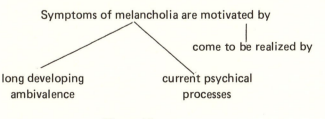

Symptoms of melancholia are motivated by

come to be realized by

long developing
ambivalence

current psychical
processes

Figure 16

roughly the same location, since the entire explication of the unconscious processes is omitted. On the positive side, the sentence retains the basic claim of the life events modeler without turning it into a Freudian process, yet still utilizes the key host model vocabulary ("object loss," "ego," "threaten," "motivate"). In short, this sentence simply brings together those overlaps that are readily apparent between the models as applied to these issues. Both talk of loss of important others from the family, of something like threats, and of the resulting depression.

This translation might be the sentence of choice in those cases where one's major ambition is to bring a sense of the source model's position or findings to the host model. It will not be very enlightening in the present case, however, since the host modeler already knows and believes this statement, on the grounds of his own model alone. At most it would be useful as a suggestion that a related finding has come about within another model, or to emphasize this aspect of melancholia for the clinician who works from the host model. If one wishes to challenge the host, give the host a rich understanding of the source, provide host-testable source claims, or help enrich the host clinician, the sentence falls short.

2. *Challenging, source-oriented*: "The conscious loss of a close family member threatens the ego, and melancholia ensues, because the person then had inadequate, few, or no object relations available."

The host modeler is challenged in this version to think in roughly the same way that the source modeler does about this claim. We use the term "challenging" rather than "threatening," "contrary," or some other term, in line with the goal we have stated throughout the book: That the translator facilitates communication, which suggests mutual exchange or debate, not contention. Thus, the host modeler is called upon to switch from the unconsciousness side of his or her own dichotomy to the consciousness side, to consider the closeness of the lost person and that the threat may result from the loss of object relations *per se* rather than from the resulting psychic process, and to think of melancholia occurring as the next step after this loss rather than as a motivated result of the loss. These are major changes for Freud's model, but they are phrased in Freud's language.

As is usual in translation of a well-packed claim, again material is sacrificed. For instance, the host sentence would be unwieldy if much more detail was included from either model, such as phrases listing all of the elements that make an event *per se* threatening (magnitude, anomie, etc.), or a negative specification of part of the Freudian process (e.g., "There need be no regression involved"). In the former case, we decided that such a listing could be omitted because, as noted earlier in our discussion, there is no agreement among life events modelers themselves about which of these components give the events their dangerous qualities. Of the latter, we felt that the negative theses are present in the translated sentence by implication and to spell them out further is only to encourage antagonism between the positions.

3. *Source-rich*: "The object loss of specific loved ones (by death of a close family member, by marital separation or divorce, or by a family member leaving home as when a child marries or a son is drafted) may fit part of your description of how melancholia operates, in those cases where the person is unable to manage the loss (say, through mourning) and the unconscious processes of melancholia take over. Often in understanding melancholia, however, one needs the kind of social focus for which Freud argued in the latter parts of his career. Specifically, the life events modelers find that the kinds of object losses noted above result in the ego finding itself alone, or apart from the community, and there is something about this relationship that apparently motivates melancholia in many of the cases."

Two critical observations are likely to occur to the reader of this translation: that the outcome is considerably more verbose than the previous translations; and that this translation is as challenging to Freud's model as is the second translation. Both of these are important disadvantages and suggest inadequacy on largely aesthetic grounds, but they do not suggest that we have failed utterly to meet the major criteria of adequacy suggested in Chapter 3 (naturalness of expression, retention of force, and balance).

This translation is challenging in a different way than the previous case, and might better be termed *expanding*. Whereas the earlier implies that Freud is wrong, this calls upon Freud's model to enlarge in order to include these additional possibilities, and leaves open both possibilities: That the Freudian model may be correct or incorrect. It comes out longer primarily because it is the first of our translations that brings along much specificity. To do so, we use a technique discussed in Chapter 2 that was unnecessary in the two earlier translations. Here the translator's voice appears, as we specifically point out to the host modelers that the move suggested is approved within their own model. This is done, however, with the use of host lexical units as much as possible, such as "melancholia" and the notion of cases rather than correlations, and where impossible with everyday language rather than source terms. One can hardly fail to note, nevertheless, that the translation does not "sound very Freudian." On our view, this suggests an important and disturbing limit to our success in this application of essentialist translation strategy. One test of the effectiveness of the technique is how well it can produce a full source claim in a host model language.

4. *Host testable*: Of these no examples are provided, since they will be of the order of one of the first three translations, simply with more care paid to how the host model tests propositions. Thus, one might convert the second translation to something like: "In case histories of melancholia one will find not that object losses result in libido regressed narcissistically from object into ego within the unconscious but that the loss is consciously threatening to ego because there are inadequate, few, or no object relations available."

In each case one will have to choose the desired balance of the models, degree of challenge and richness, and similar concerns, then add to these the need to put the translation in testable terms for the host. This latter element is no minor addition, however, since two models may test claims in quite different ways. In the present case one utilizes primarily correlational-quantitative methods and the other case histories. In other examples, the whole notion of testability may be missing in one model, or the notion of what is testable may be at odds. Indeed, some Freudians might argue that our current translation is inappropriate because Freud would not recognize an explanation of neurosis that concentrates solely on the conscious process.

5. *Clinically applicable*: "In the treatment of melancholics the psychoanalyst might focus not solely upon the psychical processes of unconscious libido regressions that result from the object loss, but also upon the nature of that object loss. This loss usually consists of the loss of a loved one and is threatening to the ego, as Freud said, but in part the threat results from the loss itself, from the isolation from other egos or the need for readjustment or skills that it brings about."

Again, this is one of many potentially appropriate translated sentences of the proposed variety. Its strengths would seen to consist in the relative absence of danger it poses to the host, amid its general success in conveying the basic life events claim. The wording suggests that the host modeler may (or may not) continue to focus primarily upon the processes of narcissism and object incorporation, but that a new concern might be added, that of the effects of the event *per se*. Within most life events model literature on this issue, the precise nature of the link between the event and depression is left unspecified. The implication is that the person's relations to social fields are changed and that this is significant. How the connection gets played out psychologically is left open, however, and there is no argument that Freud's version need be excluded.

Another way to derive an essentialist, clinically applicable translation would be to identify one seemingly well confirmed finding from the source model and translate just that limited version of the claim. Thus, one might concentrate upon the finding that it is the *exit quality* of the stressful events that produce depression, rather than the broader claim translated here.

II. An Extensionalist Translation

Introduction

Translation need not be self-conscious and formal. Just as the traveler comes to understand the names her hosts give to the things of their common environment, so the novice to some mode of describing purported instances of mental illness comes to apprehend the novel lexicon by intercourse with its speakers. Commonly the latter occurs by the application of the results of one approach to outstanding problems with another, often in published form or at conferences.

More deliberate is the introduction of a mediator into an otherwise ordinary context. Field linguists observe and record the linguistic behavior of tribal members in their everyday activities, projecting themselves *qua* competent speaker of the host language into a virtual participation in an interlinguistic dialogue with the native; out of this virtual pointing and fumbling emerges a manual of translation. For the languages of models of madness an analogous situation would be the entrance of a translator savvy in one model into a clinical setting where another model is employed. Still more fruitful would be the opportunity to observe individuals representing different models talking to each other in their native tongues, just as in some bilingual societies whole conversations are occasionally carried on in two languages. In that case the translators could determine patterns of success and failure in communication and vastly refine their understanding of the relations between expressions in the languages.

If in these contexts our translator attempts to use common extensions as the rule-of-thumb criterion for translation, incommensurabilists could indict the translation process on their familiar grounds, to the effect that although the informants *seem* to be getting along actually they are merely coexisting in different worlds. If, instead, their responses to certain representations were sought, recorded, and compared, the translator would still be an extensionalist, the linguistic "worlds" the informants function in daily may still be different, but the process of translation at least would have reference points that all can agree upon as to their general character. First, that there are actual objects of the kind known generally as thing-representations; second, that these objects include thing-representations that purportedly refer to some entities or processes that some informants believe do not exist, but insofar even nonbelievers can talk about them. Further, nonbelievers can talk about these things in ways that evince understanding of what they are supposed to be like, much like the well-informed but incredulous foreigner in attendance at a native ritual.

The extensional translator, therefore, uses representational objects as ways of fixing reference when formulating a translation both for the sake of utility and in order to forestall injecting IT into characterizations of the translation process. The latter is justified in that translations are designed according to satisfactory responses to queries in the presence of thing-representations, so minimally the translator claims that the results of such labors constitute a record of admirable construals of the thing-representations in each language. This is not to deny that more ambitious translation claims are also made, having to do with the systematic translatibility of other expressions or parts of expressions, but these, too, should ultimately be justifiable based upon the experimental scheme.

There is a further theoretical problem associated with the use of certain sorts of depictions that has not yet been addressed. Ordinarily the field translator pursuing an extensional strategy takes note of things, events, and entities, seemingly addressed by the native in his own tongue, things that are not themselves usually in any part linguistic. However, the extensional translator of models of madness may in the course of gathering information use depictions that include a linguistic component. For example, a videotape of a case history will include not only ordinary language but perhaps also some remarks by a narrator in the language of a particular model. In querying informants the translator sometimes will have to direct their attention to statements that strictly speaking are in a "foreign language," whether ordinary language or another model-language, or in the language of the present informant.

It would appear that such a factor contaminates any such depictive material the translator might wish to use to help establish applicability conditions for translation, thus reducing the extensional strategy to an absurd limitation to wordless depictions. However, so to conclude is to misunderstand the role of the language employed in such contexts. The languages spoken in depictions of, say, diagnostic interviews are from the standpoint of the extensionalist strategy part and parcel of the depictive object; for practical purposes they have no more status apart from their role in that composition than does the appearance of "5" in a Jasper Johns painting. In the context of clinical education, it's true, the language employed in many such depictions is taken as separate from the case. But in the translating process the language employed in the depiction, whether ordinary or technical, is part of the exhibition, as much a part as the pictures themselves. As extensional translators we are not primarily interested in reactions of informants to the case history but rather to the case history-depiction, and as such spoken words in any language are a feature of the depiction.

This is ensured in practice by the translator's care in directing attention of informants to the same word-and-picture *complex* in seeking applicability conditions. From the viewpoint of translational practice strictly, to ask an informant if a certain diagnosis offered in a case history-depiction is "right" is like asking an art critic if Johns' "5" in his painting is "right." In any but a narrowly aesthetic sense both questions are nonsensical, for the *assertive* "rightness" of the diagnosis has no significance for the translation being sought for, and the *assertive* "rightness" of the "5" has no significance for the effect being sought for.

Admittedly the informant's responses will sometimes partly be conditioned by some technical remark of, say, a voice-over narrator, in which case there are two possibilities: The remark is in the language of the informant, so that one expects assent to a query analogous to the remark; or the remark is not in the language of the informant, so that the informant is queried as usual in his own language, no bilingualism on the part of the informant being assumed. Even if the latter informant happens to be a bilingual, it is still the response to the scene in his primary language that we seek, and it is hard to see how his bilingualism could corrupt that response. Remarks in ordinary language, such as the responses of a patient in a depicted clinical interview, will also be taken by the translator as part of the extensional tableau, and queries of informants directed toward the word-and-picture complex.

The Translation

In an actual experimental trial informants representing the "life events" and Freudian models were queried separately while viewing a video-tape of a diagnostic interview.[65] Prior to the trials, the translator hypothesized that the source claim sentence, "Exit events play a determining part in clinical depression," could be translated into the Freudian model as "Object loss, often compensated for by identification with parental functions, is a conditioning factor in melancholia." The translator also noted some expressions associated with the expressions in the claim sentences and wrote them into diagrams, though unlike the essentialist the significance of the extensionalist's diagrams is pragmatic, helping him to trace the relationships in evaluating experimental results later on.

The crucial results with some examples can be summarized briefly. "Exit events" turned out to be applicable to depictive scenes to which "superego conflicts" (including "self-blame") and "object loss" or "perceived object loss" were applicable. For instance, when the interviewee is shown describing how, at a crucial time during a holiday season just prior to a suicide attempt, some friends left him alone in their apartment, "exit event" and "perceived object loss" were applicable. When the interviewee is shown describing how he quit his job after eight years with the same company, "exit event" and "perceived object loss" were also applicable. When he is shown describing his subsequent drifting from job to job and how his friends and his money were finally "used up," "exit event" and "self-blame" were applicable.

In the source language "social stressors" are events that are important alterations in one's personal life and can contribute to one's vulnerability to clinical depression. Depictive scenes to which "social stressor" was applicable were also those to which "superego conflicts", including "self-blame" and, to a lesser degree, "perceived object loss" were applicable. Thus, to a scene showing the interviewee's claims of increasing pressure put on him by his boss before he resigned, "social stressor" and "superego conflicts," as well as "self-blame," were applicable. This pattern was also established by responses to scenes of the interviewee relating his difficulties in finding another position, attributing this to his high level of experience and "the so-called recession," and also in his account of a friend who "brought it on himself" when he "drank himself to death."

Other instances of *paratopicality* (see Chapter 4) supporting translatability of certain expressions had to do with "chronic disorder" in the source model and "obsessional trait" in the host. However, how strong the grounds would be for a reverse translation is of course another matter. "Physical concomitant of stress" also evidenced paratopicality with "conversion symptom" at scenes of the interviewee recalling how "the pressure became physical" shortly before a suicide attempt and reporting a "tightness in my body" during the interview.

More general patterns suggesting further experimental refinements also appeared, especially during a segment in which the interviewee is shown describing the period immediately prior to his suicide attempt. The life events modeler volunteered a characterization of "a series of exits from the social field," while the Freudian modeler assented to a query-response pattern including mainly "self-blame" and "slight ambivalence."

As we expected, the results were at least as enlightening for what was *not* shown as a significant referent across models. This took the form either of an obviously poor translation or none at all. What was a depiction of "intrapsychic conflict" for the life events modeler was "disinterest, discontent," for the Freudian, clearly a more specific response in the latter than in the former even relative to each model. What was a "symptom of depression" for the life events modeler, a report of low energy levels in the mornings prior to the attempted suicide, was a "depletion of ego energy" (associated with withdrawal of ego into libido) for the Freudian. Clearly these applications, too, play very different roles within each model, the former mainly descriptive and the latter more systematically explanatory. Further, the interviewee's depicted offhand remark about "doing it with a gun" held no obvious reference for the life events modeler but elicited rapid assent to "obsessional trait" from the Freudian. On the other hand, the interviewee's depicted account of the period immediately following his resignation as "OK in the beginning" was "coping" (associated with a reentry attempt) for the life events modeler but no obvious reference for the Freudian.

Despite these qualifications the translator found good grounds for continuing along the lines of this translation. That "exit event" and "social stressor" were applicable to the same depictions as not only "object loss" and "self-blame" but also "super-ego conflicts" helps preserve in the host language the social character of those events as described in the source language. The patterns of description for each modeler of the presuicide attempt period supports the hypothesis that some referents to which "plays a determining part in clinical depression" is applicable are also those to which "is a conditioning factor in melancholia" is applicable. Combining these general results of paratopicality supports prospects for further refinements.

Of course, many more experimental trials with various depictions and informants would have to be conducted before even this limited translation could be adopted with confidence. But the results encourage one to think that such a continued project would be rewarding and practicable. One extraneous result of this experiment gave a lesson not only in translation, but also in the importance of adequate tools for fieldwork: Neither of the informants was satisfied with the videotape as a depiction of good interview technique for their respective models. "No stress history" volunteered the life events modeler; "no developmental data" volunteered the Freudian modeler, hence another translation suggested itself.

As another unanticipated but informative result, during the experimental phase with the Freudian informant the experimenter noticed some uncertainty in response to queries concerning "narcissism". Latter discussion revealed that the Freudian "dialect" of the informant had an accent on the later work in the Freudian corpus than that of the translator, for whom "narcissism" had stronger association with "ego regression" than it did for the informant. These dialects in model-languages are often related to the historic development of models, as in this case, so one could hypothesize that the relative youth of the life events model lessens the possibility of such communication breakdowns.

Naturally, the formal protocol for working with informants described in Chapter 4 breaks down to some degree in practice. For example, it may be evident to the translator that the informant should be invited to volunteer responses of her own, stressing that these should be as brief as possible. Although this seemed to work well in our experiment with extensional translation, it does mark a deviation from the query-response principle. Further trials should, therefore, incorporate the volunteered responses in the usual manner of querying. Generally, as in all such fieldwork, all responses should be recorded for later evaluation. As a practical matter, it proved important to use depictions that could be manipulated easily, as in this case where a videotape machine was frequently stopped and started again, sometimes in order to emphasize particular moments in the depiction, sometimes in order to record a lengthy or considered response. The apparent certainty of the response should also be recorded in some way, if it is either very positive or unusually hesitant.

The next step in the translation of these models of depression would require the use of a number of varied depictions and informants in order to increase confidence in the paratopicality suggested so far. Other typical statements suggested by a model must also be tested and the results incorporated into the previously well-confirmed translations. Some of the later results could indicate revisions of previous accounts, but always the purpose is to obtain as much extensional ground for the proposed translations as possible. Carried far enough, a network of interrelated translations could provide a translation manual recommending standard paratopical pairs for translations, perhaps specifying kinds of depictions that typically yield assent to each expression, as well as relevant depictive contexts qualifying these translations.

"Complete" manuals might always be only fanciful, not only for want of dedicated systematic extensional translators but also because of limitations on our ability to know the boundaries of models. Manuals of a more limited sort, specifying a modest list of paratopical expressions, would have value, however, as do modest lists of useful foreign language expressions in tourist guides.

Conclusion

In this book we have tried to address directly some possibilities that much recent literature on the nature of scientific models and their ilk has been speculating about. In so doing we have not tried to skirt any of the numerous difficulties engendered by the topic, but we have candidly qualified those premises or construals that affected the course of investigation but were not themselves received in all quarters. Our touchstone continually has been the practice of translation itself, as understood by its practitioners; continually, also, our constraints have come in the form of the differences, varying in relevance and weight, between natural language and theoretical models. We do not pretend to have established without question even the feasibility, let alone the practicality, of such novel translational activity; but we do contend that, were there accepted canons for such translation, the potential benefits of exchange among the numerous social science cultures would be enormous. Thus it has seemed a worthy subject for daring but rigorous investigation.

Somewhat less modestly, we believe that we have formulated the grounds for such procedures, though numerous problems remain before this can become a certainty. The project is hampered, for example, by our current lack of understanding of the precise nature and role of models in areas such as that of clinical psychology, especially the extent to which they are indeed akin to formal models in logic and mathematics. Further, it is to be expected that discussions concerning the relation between natural and theoretical languages will continue to be influenced by new developments in linguistics, with unforeseen consequences for our program. Many will wonder to what degree any such translation procedures can be applied to models that seem still more distant from one another than those we have canvassed in detail, such as biochemical and existential models of madness. The notion of translation, too, requires closer study in this kind of context than we have been able to give it. Perhaps the liveliest new disputes this project could encourage have to do with the grounds and mechanics of the translation strategies themselves, including especially the ways the advantages of each can be brought to bear upon the limitations of the other.

Still, what is the richness of problems with an idea is but the richness of its possibilities from another angle. We are satisfied that, at the very least, this idea engenders both.

Notes

1. Jerome K. Myers, Jacob Lindenthal, and M. Pepper, "Life Events and Psychiatric Impairment," *The Journal of Nervous and Mental Disease* 152, (1971), p. 155.

2. Judith G. Rabkin and Elmer Streuning, "Life Events, Stress, and Illness," *Science* 194, (1976), p. 1019.

3. Myers, et al., "Life Events and Psychiatric"; Rabkin and Streuning, "Life Events, Stress"; E.S. Paykel, "Life Stress and Psychiatric Disorder," in B.S. and B.P. Dohrenwend, eds., *Stressful Life Events* (New York: Wiley-Interscience, 1974); Nan Howard and Robert Scott, "A Proposed Framework for the Analysis of Stress in the Human Organism," *Behavioral Science* 10, (1965): 141–160; George W. Brown and Tirril Harris, *Social Origins of Depression* (New York: Free Press, 1978); George Brown, Tirril Harris and J. Copeland, "Depression and

Loss," *British Journal of Psychiatry* 130, (1977): 1–18; Camille Lloyd, "Life Events and Depressive Disorder Reviewed," *Archives of General Psychiatry* 37, (1980): 529–548; George J. Warheit, "Life Events, Coping, Stress and Depressive Symptomatology," *American Journal of Psychiatry* 136, (1979): 502–507; Eberhard H. Uhlenhuth and Eugene Paykel, "Symptom Intensity and Life Events," 28 (1973): 473–477; Barbara S. Dohrenwend and Bruce Dohrenwend, "Some Issues in Research on Stressful Life Events," *The Journal of Nervous and Mental Disease* 166, (1978): 7–15; Barry Glassner, C. Haldipur and J. Dessauersmith, "Role Loss and Working-Class Manic Depression," *The Journal of Nervous and Mental Disease* 167, (1979): 530–541; M.J. Leff, J. Roatch and W. Bunney, "Environmental Factors Preceding the Onset of Severe Depression," *Psychiatry* 33, (1970): 293–311; B. Mahendra, "Stress and the Major Psychiatric Illness," *Acta Psychiatry Scandinavia* 56, (1977): 161–7; and P. Clayton, J. Halikas and W. Maurice, "The Depression of Widowhood," *British Journal of Psychiatry* 120, (1972): 71–77.

4. George Brown et al., *Social Origins*; "Depression"; and "Life Events and Psychiatric Disorders, Part 2: Nature of the Causal Link," *Psychological Medicine* 3, (1973): 159–173.

5. Lloyd, "Life Events and Depressive."

6. cf., Warheit, "Life Events, Coping."

7. cf., Rabkin and Streuning, "Life Events, Stress"; and Howard and Scott, "Proposed Framework."

8. Summarized in Paykel, "Life Stress'; see also Myers, "Life Events and Psychiatric," p. 148.

9. Thomas Holmes and R. Rahe, "The Social Readjustment Rating Scale," *Journal of Psychosomatic Research* 11, (1967): 213–218.

10. Eugene Paykel, J. Myers, M. Dienelt, et al., "Life Events and Depression," *Archives of General Psychiatry* 21, (1970): 753–760; and see Paykel, "Life Stress."

11. George Brown, F. Sklair, T.O. Harris, et al., "Life Events and Psychiatric Disorders I: Some Methodological Issues," *Psychological Medicine* 3, (1973): 74–87; and see Brown and Harris, *Social Origins*.

12. Lloyd, "Life Events and Depressive."

13. N.R. Frost and P.J. Clayton, "Bereavement and Psychiatric Hospitalization," *Archives of General Psychiatry* 34, (1977): 1172–1175.

14. Alfred Dean and Nan Lin, "The Stress-Buffering Role of Social Support," *Journal of Nervous and Mental Disease* 165, (1977): 403–417.

15. Howard and Scott, "Proposed Framework."

16. Dohrenwend and Dohrenwend, "Some Issues"; and Glassner et al., "Role Loss."

17. D.P. Mueller, D. Edwards and R. Yarvis, "Stressful Life Events and Psychiatric Symptomatology," *Journal of Health and Social Behavior* 18, (1977): 307–317.

18. cf., E.G. Jaco, "The Social Isolation Hypothesis and Schizophrenia," *American Sociological Review* 19, (1954): 567–77.

19. Brown and Harris (*Social Origins*) propose a much more elaborate way to judge if life events are causal, but this has so far not been adopted broadly by life events researchers.

20. e.g., Paykel, "Life Stress"; and Myers, "Life Events and Psychiatric."

21. cf., Paykel, "Life Stress," p. 148.

22. e.g., Myrna M. Weissman and Gerald Klerman, "Sex Differences and the Epidemiology of Depression," *Archives of General Psychiatry* 34, (1977): p. 100.

23. Freud, *Complete Works*, Vol. 14, pp. 244–246.

24. *Ibid.*, p. 243 (as discussed below).

25. *Ibid.*, pp. 244 and 246.

26. e.g., J. Feigher, E. Robins, et al., "Diagnostic Criteria for Use in Psychiatric Research," *Archives of General Psychiatry* 26, (1972): 57–63.

27. Myers, "Life Events and Psychiatric."

28. Freud, *Complete Works*, Vol. 14, p. 243.

29. *Ibid.*, pp. 245 and 251.

30. Freud, *Complete Works*, Vol. 19, p. 87.

31. Freud, *Complete Works*, Vol. 14, p. 245.

32. Freud, *Complete Works*, Vol. 12, p. 262; and Vol. 7, p. 266.

33. Freud, *Complete Works*, Vol. 14, p. 245.

34. *Ibid.*, pp. 249–250.

35. *Ibid.*, pp. 251–252.

36. *Ibid.*, p. 258.

37. A possible additional candidate would be *cathexis*, but this term does little work beyond the everyday notion that psychical energy becomes attached to objects or ideas (Laplance and Pontalis, *The Language of Psychoanalysis*, New York: Norton, 1973, pp. 62–63), especially in the writings about melancholia.

38. Rycroft, *Critical Dictionary*, p. 6.

39. Freud, *Complete Works*, Vol. 14, p. 258.

40. *Ibid.*

41. Freud, *Complete Works*, Vol. 1, p. 201.

42. Freud, *Complete Works*, Vol. 14, pp. 73–102.

43. *Ibid.*, p. 249.

44. *Ibid.*, p. 252.

45. Freud, *Complete Works*, Vol. 7, p. 114.

46. Freud sees the three as connected: "... For what is older is more primitive in form and in psychical topography lies nearer to the perceptual end." (Vol. 5, p. 548).

47. This paragraph employs the analysis of Laplance and Pontalis, *The Language*, pp. 386–388.

48. Freud, *Complete Works*, Vol. 14, p. 249–250.

49. *Ibid.*, p. 252.

50. *Ibid.*, p. 257.

51. *Ibid.*, pp. 246 and 257.

52. *Ibid.*, p. 241.

53. Freud, *Complete Works*, Vol. 7, p. 276.

54. Freud, *Complete Works*, Vol. 14, p. 249.

55. e.g., *Ibid.*, p. 252.

56. *Ibid.*, p. 257.

57. Niklas Luhmann, "The Future Cannot Begin," *Social Research* 43, (1976): 130–152.

58. Freud, *Complete Works*, Vol. 17, p. 99. We wish to thank Stipe Mestrovic for contributions to this analysis.

59. Freud, *Introductory Lectures on Psychoanalysis* (London, Penguin, 1974), p. 136.

60. e.g., throughout "Psychopathology of Everyday Life."

61. Freud, *Complete Works*, Vol. 7, p. 53.

62. Freud, *Complete Works*, Vol. 11, p. 60.

63. Freud, *Complete Works*, Vol. 7, p. 266.

64. cf., Frank Cioffi, "Freud and the Idea of a Pseudo-Science," in Robert Borger and Frank Cioffi, eds., *Explanation in the Behavioral Sciences* (London: Cambridge University Press, 1970), p. 487.

65. "Mr. Paulin: Depressive Neurosis with Increased Risk of Suicide," Simulated Psychiatric Patient Interviews, Departments of Psychiatry and Medical Education, USC, 1976.

Index